PLANNING FOR SERVICE

PLANNING FOR SERVICE

An Examination of the Organisation and Administration of
Local Authority Social Services Departments

by

Robert Foren, M.A.

and

Malcolm J. Brown, Ph. D

Lecturers in Applied Social Studies
University of Bradford

CHARLES KNIGHT & CO. LTD.
LONDON
1971

Charles Knight & Co. Ltd.
11/12 Bury Street, London EC3A 5AP

Copyright©1971
Charles Knight & Co. Ltd.

SBN 85314 087 1

Printed in Great Britain by
Brown Knight & Truscott, London and Tonbridge

Contents

Foreword

by Sir Charles Barratt

AS A MEMBER of the Seebohm Committee and a former local government chief executive I commend 'Planning for Service' not only to Directors of Social Services and their senior staff but equally to the Chairmen and members of Social Services committees as a thoughtful aide memoire at a very important moment in the reorganisation and development of the local government personal social services.

The Authors very wisely have not attempted to provide an organisational blue-print nor to spell out a universal list of priorities in the search for the Seebohm Committee's 'wider conception of social service', but have provided a valuable check list covering the many issues which will inevitably arise and in addition have spelt out many of the even more difficult personal, psychological and professional problems which must be anticipated before the existing partial and fragmented effort is welded into a new whole, in the words of the former Minister of State, 'to carry out the purpose of the Seebohm Report'. What I believe the countless informal discussions both in the committee room and in the course of travelling around the country indelibly printed on the minds of the authors of that Report was a picture of the wide variation in local community needs and of attitudes towards them, of the great fluctuations in the quantity and quality of local resources of all kinds and of the significance of local socio-geographic factors in the personal social services, all of which served to emphasise the need for organisational flexibility and the scope for local experimentation in the planning and development of the new service.

Whether local authorities will find the inspiration, the stimulus and the freedom they need at this point of time in the Local Authority Social Services Act, 1970 is debatable. The unimaginative style of the statute is the price one pays for legislation deliberately drawn in the form of a consolidating measure, and what the Authors call the 'chill statement' which accompanied the original Bill – that it was not to be expected to result in any significant increase in expenditure from public funds nor to have any appreciable effect on public service manpower – was a technical 'must'. But is Section 7 of the Act, which bluntly asserts that in the exercise of their social services functions – including the exercise of any statutory discretions permitted to them – local authorities shall act under the general guidance of the Secretary of State, to be taken as a foretaste of that 'greater freedom for local authorities within the framework of national policies laid down by Parliament' and the promised 'more intimate partnership and a more effective dialogue' between Parliament and local government in the 1970s? Only in a reading of Hansard – where there seems to have been almost an open conspiracy between Government and Opposition to defeat the Rules of Parliament – can local authorities find their inspiration and evidence of a general acceptance of Seebohm philosophy.

The Authors demonstrate their conviction of the significant contribution which a new concept of the social services can make to a local authority's comprehensive community development planning and the scope for local initiative, local experiment and, above all, local leadership. One can only hope and pray that they and the many others who look forward to a major step forward in this field in the next decade will not be disappointed, and that the rigidity of the central administrative mind will not see in the reserved authority in Section 7 the opportunity to restrain the progressive local authority which sees as the aim of its social services department a truly comprehensive approach to the social problems of individuals, families and communities.

CHARLES BARRATT

Introduction

THE implementation in April 1971 of the Local Authority Social Services Act, 1970, is going to involve a large number of local authority social services committees and their newly appointed directors in a great deal of problem-solving and decision-taking. All over England and Wales individuals and groups will be endeavouring to find answers to similar questions, questions concerning the re-organisation of existing services, questions concerning the creation of new services, questions concerning policy, the redeployment of staff, of resources and of equipment, questions concerning the utilisation of buildings, the functions of residential establishments of all kinds and sizes, the organisation of in-training schemes, the recruitment of volunteers; questions concerning a hundred-and-one other matters. And answers will not come easily, nor will they necessarily be the same answers in different areas. Right answers are more likely to be found where the problems have been studied systematically against a background of relevant information concerning the present and future needs of the service area, and decisions taken which take account of the type of service, the quantity of service, the quality of service, the frequency of service and the location of service needed by the particular community or part of the community concerned. Relevant information of this kind can come from a variety of sources, as Chapter 6 of this book makes clear, but whichever sources are tapped it is important to emphasise the essential nature of 'fact finding' or 'data gathering' exercises *before* firm long-term decisions are made.

The logical sequence 'facts before decisions', however, is only a small part of a much longer sequence, and in Chapter 1 we outline in some detail the different steps which need to be taken, from the initial point of perceiving that a need exists to the provision of the service to meet it, the evaluation of the service given and the new perception of the need.

The Seebohm Committee report (97) on which the new local authority Social Services Act is based has been criticised (161) for not providing an organisational blue-print for the new departments and for not spelling out in more detail the priorities to be pursued. It is doubtful whether the Seebohm Committee could have undertaken to do this, though they may perhaps be faulted for failing to initiate any research of their own (particularly consumer research) before they proceeded to make their far-reaching recommendations for local authority social service re-organisation. The reason they gave for not doing this was that to undertake it would postpone the publication of their proposals (!).

In one sense, however, a 'global' plan may have disadvantages. Though there is undoubtedly an urgent need for decisions to be taken about the future organisation of local government and for a re-arrangement of units of local government in order that they may plan and provide services within an administrative area of a viable size and population, there is little support for the view expressed by some in evidence to the Seebohm Committee that the personal social services should be removed from the ambit of local authorities and administered by central government. The Seebohm Committee did not, in fact, discuss the merits or otherwise of the proposal, saying merely that it was outside their terms of reference, but the arguments for making the personal social services a *local* responsibility are not only historical but also functional. Different local areas do differ from each other both in the kind and extent of the social problems they throw up and this must mean also that their social priorities must also differ.

This small book does not seek to provide a blue-print for planning either. What it does seek to do is to provide Directors of Social Services and their senior staff with a logical set of guidelines for looking at their areas, for initiating change, for planning the shape of their organisation and for evaluating the services they are providing. It also provides (in the appendix) a comprehensive (though in no sense complete) coded bibliography which may assist Directors and their staffs in filling some of the gaps in essential 'specialist' knowledge which are bound to exist for most personnel newly entering an integrated department. The range of responsibilities to be given to the new departments is so wide that in every individual member of staff, from the Director downwards, there are going to be areas of ignorance, gaps in knowledge, experiential lacunae, which will need somehow to be filled. To some extent this bibliography may be of assistance, though plainly the measures discussed in Chapter 5 can in no sense be replaced by this.

Changes on the scale and of the extent and complexity which are now about to take place are unlikely to be accomplished entirely smoothly. Some friction will inevitably accompany them and Chapter 2 analyses in some detail some of the human (psychological) aspects of this problem and emphasises the need for Directors and senior staff to be aware of the nature of these difficulties and to build into their plans positive measures to mitigate them. Both the structure of the new department, discussed in Chapter 3, and the ways in which its procedures are unified, discussed in Chapter 4, will plainly affect and be affected by the fact that the organisation's staff will be comprised of human beings, not automata; the 'shape' of the organisation therefore, will need to take account not only of the need for clear channels of formal two-way communication, clear lines of command and professional accountability, as reflected in a pyramid-shaped, hierarchical, bureaucratic organisational chart, but also of the necessity for lateral communication of both a formal and informal kind within the organisation. For a long time to come, personnel are likely to have to carry a number of different roles in the agency. In the R.A.F., during the war, a Sergeant-pilot would be undisputed 'captain' of his aircraft, authorised, when flying, to give commands to personnel holding commissioned rank to whom, on the ground, he would be subordinate. In the new social services departments it is likely that roles will be determined by a large number of factors, including both the assigned 'position in the hierarchy' and possession of 'specialised expertise'.

Communication, both internally within the organisation and externally with the 'outside world', must necessarily be a matter of great importance to the consideration of which a very high degree of priority will need to be given. The Director of Social Services will at all times have to keep in mind the claims of, his responsibility toward, and the importance of maintaining good relationships with (a) his Committee; (b) his Staff; (c) the Chief Executive (Town Clerk or Clerk to the County Council); (d) other Chief Officers; (e) the Community (including, of course, all manner of voluntary organisations; and (f) last, but by no means least, the clientele of his Department (the people it exists to serve and who provide it with its only raison d'etre).

This book does not set out to examine in detail the various means by which these six different sets of relationships may be developed or regulated, it points only to the importance of paying attention to them. Some of these matters have been given consideration elsewhere (for example, in the Maud Committee Report and in the Seebohm Committee Report). Chapters 2 and 3 do however pay great attention to the matter of communication *within* the new departments, recognising that communication will need to take many forms, assume different degrees of formality and informality, and require multi-directional channels to facilitate its expression.

In-service training and in-service learning (the subject of Chapter 5) can also be regarded as forms of communication within the organisation and plainly the status they are accorded, the degree of priority given to them, the form they take and the extent to which a training 'spirit' is allowed to permeate the whole organisation will be highly influential factors in determining the extent to which the communication of knowledge, the sharing of skills and the creation of new loyalties (all essential to the building up of a truly integrated and effective social services department) can be secured. As Chapter 2 makes clear, everyone, from the Director downwards, will be in some sense a learner and it will be necessary in deciding upon the appropriate organisational 'shape' to take account of this so that opportunities to share knowledge, experience and skills (i.e. giving *and* taking) can be maximised. Insofar as the written word can aid this process, the Appendix to this book, already referred to above, may prove of help to some. It cannot, of course, claim to be exhaustive; any bibliography covering so immense a field which sought to be so would fill several large volumes; it does, however, include the important standard works in each field and a number of other useful 'signposts', and many of the books which are listed themselves contain useful bibliographies to carry the serious reader still further.

Some of the advertisements for Directors of Social Services which have appeared in the press have stressed the importance of a familiarity with 'modern management techniques'. We suspect that the lack of specificity in this blanket phrase reflects a degree of vagueness which characterises some local authorities' approach to these matters. Which particular techniques of modern management might it be desirable for Directors of Social Services to have acquired? Many of these techniques require a level of mathematical sophistication which is unlikely to be possessed by the great majority of those seeking and securing these appointments and if appointing committees were to make knowledge in this area a necessary criterion for appointment their chances of finding appropriately qualified people would be made exceedingly difficult. Moreover, many management techniques which are used in business and industry are unlikely to prove useful in an organisation whose criteria for success must necessarily be other than 'profitability'.

Nevertheless, as is argued in Chapter 4, the new social services departments will have some similarity to 'big business' both in the number of people they employ, the range of services they offer and the size of their budgets. It will therefore be appropriate – indeed necessary – for those departments to deploy such techniques of management as will enable them to maintain their own efficiency and effectiveness. This means that Directors and senior staffs will have to acquire some expertise and knowledge in this field. They will need to be able, for example, to distinguish between Cost Benefit Analysis and Cost Effectiveness; to build a system of adequate checks into their delegation procedures; to decide in what circumstances and with which grades of staff it might be appropriate to utilise algorithms; to make informed decisions as to whether to share in the computer services of the local authority, and if so for which areas of the department's work, or to maintain its records and statistics with a punched-card system within the department; and so on. Some of these matters are discussed in Chapter 4, but again this is much too large and complicated a subject to be adequately dealt with in this small book.

In thinking about the 'unification' of departmental procedures, however, there is likely to be a tendency at first merely to 'add together' all the existing procedures as they have developed in the 'constituent departments'. Insofar as it will be the Director's responsibility to maintain existing services during the period of change-over, this will probably be inevitable. Nevertheless, over a period of time, it will be necessary for a 'rationalisation' of procedures to be planned and executed, and it is with some of these matters that Chapter 4 begins to deal.

Finally, it needs to be said that the authors of this book have endeavoured to do little more than make a small contribution to the widespread thinking and planning that must now be going on around this whole subject, examining some of the problems inherent in the setting up of the unified social services departments and suggesting what they conceive to be a rational approach and structure. As university lecturers, they do not themselves possess first-hand experience of working in local government and they may, therefore, have perpetrated occasional solecisms for which they ask indulgence in advance. They have had considerable help from a number of people whom they wish to thank very warmly and gratefully; the many imperfections in the book which remain must, however, be their own responsibility.

The next few years are going to be both daunting and exciting for all those people in the local authority social services departments who will be blazing a new trail for social work in this country and combining, perhaps for the first time, a rational and a humane approach to a very wide spectrum of individual and family problems. To that very large 'army' of field staff, residential workers, day centre personnel and social work administrators who are going to continue to 'do battle' on society's behalf, we humbly dedicate this little book, but in particular we should like to single out for especial thanks for his considerable help and support in its writing, Mr. M.F. Beglin, Director of Welfare Services in Bradford. Our thanks are also due to Mr. Peter Bye of the Lancashire County Council Children's Department, Miss G. Crabtree of the Bradford Children's Department, Miss Margaret Howe of the Leeds Children's Department, Mr. Peter Westland of the London Borough of Wandsworth Children's Department, who all provided material or assisted in other ways in getting across to two very ignorant University lecturers some of the intricacies and complexities of local authority practice and procedure in the provision of welfare.

The authors wish also to acknowledge their indebtedness to the Local Government Training Board for permitting them to use the algorithm chart (shown as Fig. 6 on page 64) which, with a series of other charts, they have produced as an experiment. The development of these charts may be extended in due course by the Board to cover the procedural application of other legislation relevant to Departments of Social Services.

Our thanks are also due to Mr. Michael Lear, cartographer in the University of Bradford, who drew a number of the illustrations for us, and we must also acknowledge the fact that the Tavistock Institute of Human Relations have kindly permitted us to reproduce short passages from *The Changing Culture of a Factory;* that Messrs. A.B.P. International have given us permission to quote from A.K. Rice's book *The Enterprise and its Environment;* and that Messrs. George Allen and Unwin have authorised us to reproduce the passage from Margaret Brown's paper in *New Developments in Casework.* Chapters 2 and 3 are based upon articles published by the authors in *The British Hospital Journal and Social Service Review* (364) and the *Local Government Chronicle* (359). To the editors of these two journals we also express our thanks.

Finally, we must express our gratitude to Muriel Brown and Elizabeth Elford for the skill and equanimity with which they have, in typing successive drafts, reduced our often quite illegible manuscript to some semblance of respectable intelligibility.

Bradford,   R.F.
October, 1970   M.B.

This book was already set up in type and the page proofs corrected when the news of the death of Sir Charles Barratt reached us. This is neither the time nor the place to record his obituary but we would not wish our gratitude to him for his generous Foreword to go unsaid. As a prominent member of the Seebohm Committee with a long and distinguished record behind him of public and local authority service, he will be long remembered and revered. His death at the age of 60 is a loss to us all.

                                                                        R.F.
February, 1971   M.B.

A FRAMEWORK FOR A
SOCIAL SERVICE ORGANISATION

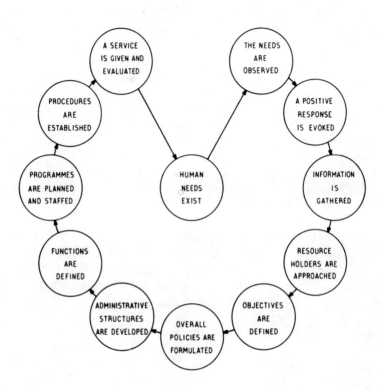

1. A Framework for Planning

A MAJOR problem facing any social work administrator is the handling of a substantial number of diverse areas of activity, each requiring a breadth of knowledge and innumerable skills in which he himself needs to have, if not some competence, at least considerable understanding, and which need to be brought together into an integrated whole.

If it is accepted that in the field of social service provision there are these wide areas of knowledge, and this multiplicity of specific skills which need to be integrated, then it follows that it is desirable that a balance be maintained between the various factors, and a logical order discovered or decided upon in which they might be brought together and institutionalised in a viable organisation.

The new departments, with few exceptions, will be large, complex organisations employing or drawing upon the expertise of representatives from a number of professions, utilising knowledge from several disciplines and deploying a variety of skills over a wide area of activity. In such a situation it is all too easy to allow the underlying philosophy that initially characterised and informed the decision to set up new types of service-giving agencies to become eroded and, in focussing upon means, to lose sight of the ends that were to be pursued.

It may therefore be salutory to remind ourselves of the logical relationship which exists and needs to be maintained between means and ends within the context of a service-giving organisation. This is presented diagrammatically in Figure 1.

In this diagram the needs of the clientele of the agency are placed in the centre. The needs of the client or family are necessarily central to the agency's existence – if they did not exist then the agency need not. And in putting them at the centre of the model we remind ourselves of the paramount importance of so arranging our procedures and our processes of organisational development that they are at all times truly client-centred.

Human needs, of course, change, as does society's perception of what constitutes need. Attention has been given in past decades to physical needs, such as food, clothing, shelter and the avoidance of bodily abuse. More recently, greater recognition and attention has been given to emotional needs, and there are indications that community participation in determining and resolving social problems may be given greater emphasis in the future.

The circumstances in which the observation of needs takes place may range from the assertive seeking-out of, or reaching-out to, those in need by social workers or other representatives of society, to the assertive seeking-out of help by those in need by mobilising themselves to force an awareness of unmet need upon society. Once an awareness of the existence of a human need is felt then some response can be evoked. If this response is other than concern then nothing further (toward meeting the need) is likely to happen. In some countries, and in some situations, basic human needs are responded to with indifference or feelings of helplessness, both of which leave basic human problems unchanged and human needs unmet.

If concern *is* evoked, this can provide the motivation to move in and seek to meet the need, and the remaining stages in the model may be by-passed. Unless one is dealing with real emergencies, however, it is probably wise, when a need is perceived which evokes concern, to move on to the next stage of the model – that of acquiring information which will enable one to have greater understanding of the true nature and extent of the need. For in the absence of adequate information, any attempt at service-giving is likely to be arbitrary and inefficient. In some areas of its activities, it is still true to say that the social work profession continues to act very much like a 'first-aider' in that it makes little effort to obtain greater understanding of the true nature and extent of the human needs it is seeking to meet. This is partly the result of the fragmented nature of the services now being replaced by the new integrated departments. There is nothing wrong

2

with giving first-aid; in a situation where first-aid is required
(e.g. in an emergency) it is, by definition, the appropriate
thing to do, but first-aid rarely, if ever, wholly meets a need
and to take the matter further must necessarily involve the
seeking of more information. Information can be sought on
both a micro- and a macro-level; i.e. about individual cases
and about 'cases in general', So far as the latter are concerned,
information needs to be gathered in relation to the social
problems that exist, both quantitatively and qualitatively, for
the area for which the agency has responsibility and some
individual or sector of the new department will need to be
familiar with appropriate methods of data-collection and be
able to present them in a meaningful way if the next stages in
the model are to be fully utilised. (This kind of agency-based
research is discussed more fully in Chapter 6.) The department
needs too, to be knowledgeable about the history of the
social problems it is concerned with, the attempts that have
previously been made to deal with them and the effectiveness
of different techniques that may have been applied to deal
with them.

It may well be the case that the roles of the observer of a
human need, the positive responder to that need and the
information gatherer will not be contained in any one single
person. It is almost certain that no individual would hold
sufficient resources to meet that need on his own. Almost
without exception, holders of financial resources, or those
having access to or authority over money, need to be
approached and involved before the sequence from the
observation of need to the giving of service has gone too far.
In local authority departments the great bulk of the finances
involved will be obtained through the machinery of local
government committees. This need not necessarily preclude
approaches to other resource holders for specific purposes –
and in particular the holders of charitable funds and voluntary
manpower who might be prevailed upon to enrich the services
given.

As money is seldom given without strings, the defined
objectives for the giving of service are likely to be something
of a compromise between those anxious to get a programme
going and those who are going to meet its cost or contribute
in some way. Any objectives formulated prior to the approach
to finance holders may therefore have to undergo some modi-

fication and the objectives that set the rest of the model into action are likely to be those that come after the 'approach to finance' stage. It is most important, however, that the objectives of a service-giving agency are clearly formulated and that priorities are determined. Social work agencies *can* function without clearly understood objectives and it is probably not being too unkind to suggest that some of them do, but if all activity is to be both effective and efficient, then clearly spelled-out objectives are necessary and it is likely that they are best defined at this stage in the sequence. Certain management techniques can help in formulating agency objectives, particularly in that they necessitate some basic thinking as part of the process of their application. The driving force, however, to any activity in this field is the underlying philosophy in relation to the assessed human needs, the measure of support given to that philosophy and the formulation of objectives which are consonant with it.

Once our objectives are clearly defined, policies in line with them can be formulated. In the absence of objectives, policies are likely to be limited to the provision of ad hoc services, because government legislation require that they be provided, rather than related specifically to an appreciation of the total needs of an area or the wish to provide a truly comprehensive service. Where services are given as a requirement of central government enactments, their intervention into the sequence is likely to be experienced at this stage. It is unlikely that the government will have examined the needs of a specific district or defined overall objectives in detail, and it is important, therefore, if functions *are* dictated, that policies to implement them be legitimately contained within the agency's overall objectives, such objectives being amended, where necessary, in order to embrace the imposed requirements.

The stages outlined thus far are likely substantially to influence the administrative structures that are developed. The conditions under which money is obtained, as well as the structure of local government itself, are likely to require that the structure for carrying the service be of a hierarchical, pyramid-shaped, bureaucratic kind, with clearly defined areas of responsibility and authority, formal lines of communication, and so on. This organisational 'shape' and the reasons for recommending it, are discussed in Chapter 3.

4

Once the structure has been decided upon, the next step is to allocate authority and responsibility to positions within it, ensuring that the division of labour is a rational one and that the functions attaching to each position are clearly defined. So far as the senior positions in the hierarchy are concerned, these functions are discussed in broad outline in Chapter 3.

The implementation of policy requires that, functions having been defined within the structure, programmes be planned and staffed. It is likely that departments will decide upon an initial programme which will make the maximum use of existing staff and material resources – it would plainly not be sensible to attempt to turn all one's residential staff into fieldworkers and vice-versa, or adapt all one's children's homes for occupation by the elderly. The influence of policy upon structure and upon programme planning is fairly obvious. If policies emphasise casework services (to choose a banal example) then small interviewing rooms rather than large ones will be required; if group-work, then somewhat larger rooms; if both, then rooms of differing sizes; if community development, then a large proportion of young energetic workers, and raincoats and wellington boots! If an increased proportion of children in care are to be fostered, then fewer residential homes need be planned. If the policies stress decentralisation, then a number of area offices throughout the district, strategically placed according to the determined needs of the various neighbourhoods (373) will be indicated.

Within each administrative structure, individuals will be attached to various roles and functions will be allocated by means of some appropriate division of labour which will itself be substantially influenced by the structure, the policies, the objectives, the human needs that exist and the means believed to be best ways of meeting them. It may be necessary to 'co-opt' some staff (e.g. specialist psychiatric consultancy facilities) on a sessional basis, to employ other staff (e.g. in residential establishments) on a part-time basis, to recruit some people on a voluntary basis, and large numbers of field and residential staff on a whole-time basis. The proportions of different types of staff and different types of appointment will doubtless depend both upon availability as well as on function, but it is at this stage in our model that attention is given to the question of staff recruitment and training.

5

Once the agency has developed its programme plan, attention needs to be given to the procedures that are most appropriate for programme fulfilment. Decisions need to be taken as to the day-to-day procedures such as those concerned with the reception of clients, the methods by which records are to be kept, staff supervised, children clothed and communication with other local authority departments and the community maintained or developed. Some of these matters are discussed in Chapter 4. In developing agency programmes, the agency Head may wish to utilise some of the techniques developed by management specialists, such as 'management by objectives' and 'planned programme budgeting'. These too are discussed in Chapter 4.

As the actual giving of service is undertaken largely by officers on the lowest stratum of the hierarchy (i.e. the social workers and residential workers, the day-centre staff, home-helps and ancillary staff who are in face-to-face contact with clients and seek to meet their needs on behalf of the agency), it is important that, through a variety of means, such staff should be encouraged and enabled to identify themselves wholeheartedly with the agency's philosophy and, as the agency's eyes and ears, contribute to the development of ever more appropriate and effective procedures for expressing it. Any opinions held as to the quality of service that is currently given seem to rest largely on the individual and subjective observation and judgement of the providers of service rather than on empirical evidence gathered in a systematic way. This is a most neglected area of social work. Not only do we tend not to evaluate service, except in the most superficial and inadequate way, we are also guilty, as a profession, of neglecting to develop the instruments by which such evaluations can be made. The difficulties involved in seeking to measure things that are not readily measurable is appreciated, but this difficulty should spur us to greater efforts and not be accepted as a reason for giving up trying, as most social service agencies have been wont to do.

In the very process of giving a service an agency acquires information about changing needs, about unmet needs or needs that are being met inadequately. All too often it has been someone outside professional social work who has highlighted the gaps in social service provision or identified groups in the community whose needs have been overlooked. This is an area of activity that needs to be developed by the social work profession itself; social service departments will have to take steps not only to obtain *greater* knowledge of the geographical area for which they have responsibility but also to make much more use of the knowledge they already have. An agency should, by acquiring and *organising* its knowledge, come to a greater *understanding* of the needs of its clientele (and its potential clientele) and it should know the extent and quality, as well as the effectiveness, of the services that it is giving. Evaluation (and constant self-criticism) should characterise all levels of a service-giving organisation. Quite apart from its value to the consumers and future consumers of the services, such an on-going exercise can also have tremendous value in terms of staff development, enabling staff to sharpen their perceptions and develop greater sensitivity.

Much research into aspects of social service provision has been undertaken from outside and social workers have tended either to ignore it or to criticise it or to seek to explain it away by suggesting that it seeks answers to questions that no-one is asking. There may be some justification for social workers resenting research activities conducted from outside – before a sociologist can helpfully undertake research for the social worker he needs to have some knowledge of social work – but the logical alternative is for the social worker to add research methods and techniques to his own professional repertoire, and some schools of social work are now equipping their students to do just this.

Agency-based research needs to be a continuing evaluation process and this means that Social Services Departments need to build research facilities into their structures from the outset.

It should not be assumed, however, that research is the only means by which evaluation of service can be undertaken. The continuing evaluation of services within a Department is a highly complicated matter which should ideally permeate the whole organisation rather than seem to be the concern of a small research unit within it. Figure 7 on page 68 shows the complex relationships which may exist between different aspects of the provision and evaluation of services for the elderly; they would not have been less complicated had we chosen services for children or the mentally handicapped.

The several stages in the process of service-giving have been set out in what is conceived to be a rational sequence. This is not to say that this is the only sequence, or that in any one case it will not be appropriate for several stages to be telescoped or tackled simultaneously. It is unlikely that in the 'real world' aspects of human activity, knowledge, skills, plans and dreams can be parcelled up as tidily as is here suggested. To-ings and fro-ings along the way will be inevitable. The model presented is a dynamic as well as a circular one.

What is clear, however, is that it is unlikely that any stage of the process that has been described can be ignored without detriment to the whole and that there should ideally be a proper balance preserved between the several parts. Currently the giving of service is often stressed at the expense of evaluating it, of properly ascertaining needs, or of examining agency objectives, policies and procedures in any really systematic way. The use of the model may play some part in helping agency heads to maintain an overall perspective and to ensure that all the factors involved in the giving and evaluation of a service are given their due consideration.

2. Human Factors in
Planning for Change

THE Mallaby Committee (96) defined 'management' as 'getting things done through other people' and saw the manager's task as involving, among other things, 'the organisation and harmonising of the work of various individuals and groups of *people'*. Which of the great psychologists it was who first coined the immortal line 'There's nowt so queer as folk' is not known, but most readers of this book will doubtless have reason to remember occasions when its truth was made more than abundantly clear to them! Harmonising the work of robots, co-ordinating the work of machines, organising the work of a computer may throw up certain problems, but compared with organising, co-ordinating and harmonising the work of individuals and groups of *people,* it is child's play. Social workers, it has to be said, are especially difficult to 'manage'. It is not so much their personalities as the nature of the job they do that we have in mind. The special problems which seems to be inherent in the nature of the relationship between the professional or semi-professional worker and the bureaucracy of which he forms a part have been pointed out by Blau and Scott (124) and Andrew Billingsley (333). These problems are likely to grow more acute as social work organisations grow larger and more complex and as the gap inevitably widens between first-line social workers who are in direct contact with clients and the top-level administrators higher up the hierarchy.

This is not, however, the basic theme of this Chapter, though it contributes to it. What we are here concerned with are the human factors in the situation of change – with what change involves and with how we react to it. The first point to be made when considering the changes ahead of us is that

9

the phrase 'the new departments' is being widely used as a kind of shorthand for the local authority social services departments which are being set up – and this can be misleading. In one sense, of course, these departments will be new; that is to say, their organisational structure will be new, their name will be new, their legal status will be new, some of their functions will be new, and so on. But they will not be new in the sense that they have no history, no antecedents, no past, they will not be new (nor could they be) in the sense that the personnel who staff them are new and freshly-minted *people.* They will not be new in the sense that most of their clients will be new. This may be very trite and obvious, but it is necessary to make the point because it is here, at the interface between what is new and what is not new, that many of the psychological problems may arise. Learning a new task may be difficult for some people; having to *unlearn* some things first may make such a task even more difficult. Much will depend upon our own attitudes, our readiness to change our ways, the extent to which we are able to adapt and apply positively what is useful and to discard what is not.

Buildings, equipment, physical resources, money – all these things are essential if the personal social services are effectively to be made available to those requiring them, but the most important resource of all is (be definition) *personnel* – fieldworkers, residential workers, day-centre staff, ancillary workers, administrators, committee members. And although all these will come together in a differently-shaped, larger yet more complex, and hopefully streamlined organisation which is appropriately geared to the attainment of its objectives, none of these people should be perceived as tabula rasa – as a 'clean slate'. Each will come to the new situation with memories and attitudes, skills and experience, preconceptions and prejudices, knowledge and beliefs, hopes and fears. disappointments and enthusiasms, old loyalties and new expectations. Some will have been former members of what may be called the 'constituent departments' within the same local authority, some will have come from similar departments in other authorities, some perhaps may be new to local government service, but all must necessarily come with a particular orientation. And this will be true too of the committee member who was perhaps previously a Children's Committee Chairman or a Welfare Services Committee Chairman. Not only may he come to the new situation with attitudes formed by his earlier orientation, he may also find that he is no longer a chairman, and have feelings about that too!

A great many 'organisational charts' have been published, and many others have doubtless been drawn up for their own purposes by local authorities in different parts of the country. We make no apology for adding to the proliferation by including our own in the next Chapter, but of course we all know that such graphical representations, though useful in many ways, can never be more than a very approximate picture of any real-life situation as it exists, or even of the situation as we would like it to be. The 'manifest', the 'assumed' and the 'extant' organisational structures will all be different, one from the other (131) (153). However we draw our charts, each role position will be filled, not by an automaton, but by a *person;* persons are complicated organisms; they cannot be relied upon to act consistently; we cannot expect of them that they will exactly fill the roles assigned to them and no more; we cannot expect of them that the relationships they have with other persons will be exactly the kind of relationships dictated by our charts, no more and no less. As human beings we applaud the fact that this is so; it is the weakness of much bureaucratic theory that it is too *rational.*

One of the authors of this book has elsewhere shown (340) how an agency worker may underfill his prescribed role, or overfill it in a variety of ways – often at the expense of his efficiency in his job – but is it really possible, in completely human terms, ever to fully prescribe another's **role**? Outside of a slave economy or a rigid prison system – and perhaps not even then – it is not feasible completely to draw boundaries around a person's activities so that they exactly fit. In practice it is likely that we shall either draw them so widely that he is bound in some way to underfill his role, or so narrowly that he feels constricted and is tempted to overfill it.

The shape of the new organisation to which the individual worker is going to be required somehow to adapt is discussed in detail in the next Chapter; for the moment let us concentrate on what the worker is going to bring with him to that new situation. With a few exceptions, the persons who will comprise the new departments will have had training for and/or experience within some other social work agency. It may be that the other agency (child care, mental health, welfare services, perhaps health, education or housing) was a department within the same local authority (what we have termed a 'constituent department'), or it may be that some of them will have come from social work agencies, or even fresh from training, elsewhere. Some of them will feel enthusiastic about and welcoming of what has been somewhat inaccurately called the 'implementation of Seebohm', others will be less so; but even for those who have campaigned for such changes there will be some uncertainties about taking on new roles, or disappointments that their expectations are not being fully realised. (Moreover, there is a tendency in many of us, when seeking change, unconsciously to assume that it is other people who must change, not ourselves; we are more ready, that is to say, to see others coming to share our own orientation than we are to modify our own.)

But the administrative changes foreshadowed by the Local Authority Social Services Act, if they are to be successfully implemented (i.e. translated into *action*), will necessarily have to be accompanied by quite radical changes in the psychological attitude and professional orientation of each member of the social services department from the Director downward. That there will be some resistances to these changes is almost inevitable – resistances which range from the consciously 'political' at one end of the spectrum to the unconsciously 'psychological' at the other. An understanding of these resistances and of the defence mechanisms to which they will give rise may, however, enable the potential friction they could generate to be prevented, ameliorated or mitigated to some extent.

Unless the anxieties provoked by change are recognised and alleviated then one must expect hostility toward the agent of change to result. As this Chapter is being written the Directors of the new departments are being sought and appointed. We now know that, subject to any special exceptions, they must all be in post by the 1st April, 1971 (113). Few readers can have been unaware of the interest, not to say anxiety, which has surrounded the whole selection process, can have been unaware of the speculation and rumour which has abounded, or can have been unconscious of the hyperactivity of the 'grapevine'. It has not been just a matter of tremendous import for the contenders for these lucrative and powerful positions – for those who were successful and for those who, having entered the lists, were wined, dined, interviewed and rejected. It has been, and still is, a matter of considerable interest for those lesser mortals, the fieldworkers, the residential workers, the middle-management, the nursery nurses, the home-helps, the secretaries, receptionists and clerks – all anxious to know who their new boss was to be and what he is going to be like.

Impending change necessarily creates a degree of uncertainty which, in its turn, can provoke anxiety. Impending large change creates larger uncertainties and greater anxiety can be generated. What kind of changes, then, may await staff members and demand a measure of adjustment? It is not merely a matter of who the boss is going to be, but of lots of other, perhaps less remote and more personal changes for each individual. So far as field-staff are concerned, we may list them as follows and then proceed to discuss each in turn:

1. changes of role and title;
2. changes of function;
3. changes of caseload;
4. changes of geographical area;
5. changes of 'work-scene' (base);
6. changes of colleagues (membership of new team);
7. changes of leader;
8. changes of clientele;
9. changes of agency policies;
10. changes of agency procedures;
11. changes of professional orientation; and
12. changes of organisational 'size'.

We have said that we propose to discuss each of these types of change in turn but, of course, many of them are interdependent and over-lapping. Moreover, there is another point first to be made. One can envisage, in different circumstances, a single worker changing his job and going to work for a different, larger, agency – a probation officer, shall we say, two or three years ago, moving into child care in a big city from a small probation office in mid-Wales. In such a case all the twelve types of change listed above would apply to him, but they would apply in a subtly different way from the situation which will obtain as the new departments come into existence. Such a worker changing his job might, as has been said, have many adjustments to make, but at least our ambitious Welsh probation officer will have been entering an ordered world with firm procedures, established methods of working and personnel who knew their jobs to whom he could turn for advice or direction. This will not be the case for the individual entering the new integrated social services department, since there will not exist, to begin with, any firm procedures, established methods of working, or personnel who know their jobs. It will not be an ordered world. Indeed each individual within it will be in like case, each will feel disorientated; none will know quite where to turn for stability. In such an unstable situation there will be a tendency to cling to what one knows; that is to say, to look to the past for guidance – and this may be wise. But it *may* be unreliable, for in a strict sense past experience may only be relevant to past situations, and, as in a chess problem, when one piece is moved the relationship which exists between all the other pieces is also changed. It may be wiser to look to the future for guidance than to look back to the past. It may be more appropriate to decide one's actions in terms of their likelihood to achieve a future goal, to which the organisation and all concerned in it are committed. But this may be easier said than done; knowing *what* one wants to achieve is not always to know *how* to set about getting it.

Of course, in thus expressing it, we are over-simplifying and exaggerating. Things will not be so chaotic as we have made them out to be, nor will the new organisation be so anarchic and rudderless as we have pretended. Some (indeed much) of our past experience will, of course, still be useful, necessary, essential and appropriate. Many of the jobs which had to be done before will still have to be done (indeed it will be a responsibility of the department during the period of reorganisation to maintain existing services). Skills one has learned, knowledge one has acquired, principles one has embraced – all these will not have to be abandoned as useless in a new situation, because many new situations will look very much like the old situations did. But we are purposely exaggerating in order to point to the *nature* of the problems. Large-scale structural change can and will produce subjective feelings in many of those involved of disorientation and confusion. It may be that for any one individual not all the twelve types of change listed above will apply, but many of them will – though to different degrees, with different emphases, occasioning different amounts of stress – and it is important that we should be aware of them.

Change of role and title

The first type of change in our list was that of role and title. At the present time no-one knows how quickly the administrative changes which are envisaged will be fully accomplished. There will almost certainly be some gradualism about them, in the sense that time must elapse, following the appointed day, before, shall we say, the concept of the 'general purpose social worker' becomes a reality. Nevertheless, within a relatively short space of time, departments will have so organised themselves that cases will have been re-distributed and, with some exceptions, families receiving social work help of some kind will be served by a 'single worker'. This presumably means that titles like 'child care officer' and 'mental welfare officer' will disappear and each fieldworker will acquire a caseload which, although to begin with may comprise a high proportion of the kind of case he formerly used to deal with exclusively, will gradually become more 'mixed'. This means that each worker will have to become a 'different kind of professional person' and have to adjust to new agency expectations. This will also involve observing others having to make changes too, and it may be that considerations of relative status between oneself and others may become an issue, as may also, to begin with, some anomalous pay differentials. But aside from 'practicalities' of this kind, we should not too quickly shrug off the importance to an individual of changes in role and title, for it is in these that his *professional identity* may be said to reside and be given meaning and purpose.

Change of function

Closely related to problems of this kind are those subsumed under our second type of change - *changes of function.* Changes of this kind almost certainly involve the necessity to acquire new skills and may perhaps seem to imply the derogation of existing ones. Both factors have important implications for us. The necessity to acquire new skills may be seen by some as opportunity; by others it can feel very threatening. How are these new skills to be acquired? We cannot send everyone away on a course – particularly at a time when our new agency is under so many pressures. Might there perhaps be alternative methods available to us for the transmission of new skills? Some of these possibilities are discussed in Chapter 5, but however we approach the matter, we must be careful to place value on old skills and not to derogate them. In a situation such as is envisaged, it may well be the case that as everyone is in some sense a learner, he may also be a teacher, and we should seek ways and structures for the *exchange* and *sharing* of skills. It must also be recognised that changes of function can present difficulties for an individual which are quite other than those of acquiring knowledge and skills. His feelings and attitudes are also an important factor, and it may well be the case that for some individuals there will be especial difficulties if they are required to work with particular groups of clients; for some, mental illness or physical handicap or senility, to quote three examples at random, can arouse such strong feelings as to make it extremely difficult for them, without considerable help, to undertake any professional work at all.

Change of caseload

In saying this we have moved into our third type of change – for closely allied to changes of function are *changes of caseload*. What does the acquisition of a more 'mixed' caseload mean? At worst it could mean the extension of inappropriate methods of help over an even more widely disparate range of clients than before, and we may recall that vivid passage in Margaret Brown's important paper: 'A Review of Casework Methods (in 326):

'Do we adopt a rather stereotyped approach with everyone – anxious mother, delinquent youth, ambulatory schizophrenic alike – or do we vary in the relationships we establish? Are we always permissive and accepting, or (benevolently) authoritarian? Do we habitually listen passively, encourage the expression of feelings, explore our clients' early backgrounds; or is our tendency to take an active part in interviews, offering advice and suggestions, and setting limits? It is so much easier to observe the characteristic approaches of our colleagues in casework than to know our own.'

Workers are going to have to learn to be a great deal more

versatile and less idiosyncratic; they are going to have to learn
to deal with people less by reference to the administrative
category into which they seem to fall; less too in accordance
with their own personality needs; and more in terms of their
clients' real needs and the nature of the social situations in
which their clients find themselves. This is going to call for
very much improved methods of social diagnosis and the
provision of supervisory and consultative support of a high
order. A mixed caseload will mean more variety in the
individual worker's work and less 'routine' – a change which
can be both welcome and unwelcome to the individual concerned. It will also call for a much broader knowledge base –
someone who has previously specialised in working, shall we
say, with the elderly and the handicapped, will now need to
have some understanding of the needs of (and the law
relating to) deprived and delinquent children and the mentally
subnormal; a worker experienced in child care will now have
to develop some expertise in the aftercare requirements of
the schizophrenic spinster discharged from psychiatric hospital to the care of her elderly parents.

Change of geographical area

The fourth kind of change we listed was that of the
geographical area. This will not, of course, affect everyone,
but a rational re-deployment of personnel resources must
inevitably mean moving some workers from sectors of a city,
or even a county, which are familiar to them, to other sectors
which are less so. A change of this kind is, of course, more
likely to influence the effectiveness of a social worker than
of most other persons changing their geographical location,
since aside from the obvious personal influences the environment exercises, an intimate knowledge of the area in which
he works is essential to a social worker if he is to understand
the problems of his clients who live there and have effective
working relationships with other key people in the community
– police, school-teachers, youth leaders, voluntary workers,
community workers, landladies, employers, to name but a
few.

Change of 'work scene' and colleagues

Closely connected to the problems for the worker of
changing his geographical area are the problems of changing

his work-scene, or office, and experiencing a change of colleagueship and team-membership. The social worker's workshop is the familiar room in which he conducts many of his interviews, in which he plans his work, in which he records and thinks about it. Because of the nature of his job, his constant involvement in the problems of others, his close association with people in difficulty, people who are handicapped or sick, people who are feckless, or helpless, dependent and over-demanding, the social worker has considerable need to feel a sense of team-membership, professional acceptance and belongingness. For most workers, whatever their occupation, the work-group is important; in social work its importance is even more considerable.

Change of leader

Membership of a new work-team may also involve a *change of team-leader,* and this too can be more than superficially disconcerting. Such a change may involve a number of inter-related but separate factors of which none should be overlooked. First, it may mean losing, i.e. separating from, the leader one formerly worked under, and if a good supervisory relationship existed with him. then one is going to have feelings about having compulsorily to end it. Secondly, it may mean having to adjust to and accept the new leader - someone, perhaps one is going at first to perceive as alien, as different, as embracing a somewhat different professional discipline, orientation and background from one's own. Thirdly, because he too is 'new to the job' he may be seen to be much less reliable than one could wish in a leader; he is going to be a person, perhaps, who will have to carry much of one's negativism and resentment about so much change, about so much initial chaos. He will be the one who will be issuing instructions (many of them inevitably unwelcome); the one who is 'responsible' for one's own feelings of disorientation and confusion. And he will be the leader of a team of which one may not feel oneself to be completely a part - a leader known to some of one's new colleagues far more intimately than to others, or to oneself. Lastly it is worth mentioning that he may be a 'changing leader'. To quote A.K. Rice (272):

'Under conditions of change, the preoccupation of leaders with the most difficult areas of task performance can create difficulties for their followers as well. As the problem area changes so will a leader's attention. Provided followers accept their leader's interpretation of the dominant need of the enterprise, they may still be content to follow; but when either their interpretation differs, or they find solutions to the fresh problems beyond their capacity, they may be distressed and resentful at what they feel as abandonment . . .'

Change of clientele

The eighth type of change we listed as *change of clientele.* This is different from change of caseload (number three in our list) in that it is much more personal. We are concerned here with the problems of the worker, not in adapting to different *kinds* of client, different administrative categories, a more heterogeneous group of clients,˙but with the worker's feelings about *actual people,* about having to give up working with old Mrs. Smith one has been visiting regularly for eighteen months and having to hand over the case to somebody else, maybe somebody one does not even know, or whose ability to cope with it is to some extent suspect. Conversely, there will also be problems for the worker in having to take on other clients – lots of them perhaps – whom it is going to take a long time to get to know – clients, moreover, who may well feel angry or depressed at losing the familiar worker *they* used to have.

Change of policies and procedures

Changes 9 and 10 concern *changes of policies and procedures,* and as a number of our readers are likely to be senior social work administrators, we will not expatiate on these kinds of changes beyond emphasising the need when thinking about introducing changes of policy and changes of procedure to think not only of the policy itself, or the new procedure itself, satisfying ourselves and our committee that it is the right policy, that it will achieve its objectives, that the objectives themselves are the right ones to pursue, and so on, but also to think about such important questions as the impact of the new policy upon the people who are going to have to implement it, or who are going to be affected by it in some way. How is the policy to be introduced, how is it to be communicated, how is it to be explained, how is it to be justified? How will it be perceived by some members of staff;

what is the likelihood of it being misunderstood? In what way might it affect working conditions? In what way might it deviate from professional philosophies? Will such a policy or procedure involve the provision of additional training facilities? If it is not likely to be a popular measure, will it be implemented in a 'ritualistic' manner which robs it of any likelihood of effectiveness? All these questions – and there are many other similar questions which need to be asked – should be carefully considered and correctly answered before introducing changes of policy or major changes in procedures. They would be necessary in a steady-state organisation; they are vital in the kind of situation we are here discussing. In the fluid, not very stable conditions of an organisation-struggling-to-become there will also be a tendency perhaps to introduce off-the-cuff ad hoc procedures to suit the needs of the moment. This can be very disconcerting to a staff desperately in need of stability because such decisions by their very nature have frequently to be changed, and senior staff should, therefore, do all in their power to avoid making too many of these temporary, ill-considered and expedient decisions, though it is recognised that to begin with some will be inevitable.

Change of professional orientation

The penultimate type of change in our list is *change of professional orientation,* and we have already referred in passing to this when discussing some of the others. We have listed it separately, however, because it needs to be emphasised that more is involved than giving up being exclusively a child care officer and becoming a mental welfare officer too, or whatever it may be. If this were all such a change involved then there would be something wrong. To see it in these terms is to misunderstand the Seebohm Committee Report. Creating the new departments is not just a matter of putting all the social workers together and sharing out the cases more economically. The spirit of the Seebohm Committee recommendations requires that we should adopt a new way of looking at social need, a new way of looking at clients, a new way of looking at the community, a new way of looking at social service provision. Let us remind ourselves of what the Committee said in paragraph 474 of its Report:

'At many points in this Report we have stressed that we

see our proposals not simply in terms of organisation but as embodying a wider conception of social service, directed to the well-being of the whole of the community and not only of social casualties, and seeing the community it serves as the basis of its authority, resources and effectiveness. Such a conception spells, we hope, the death-knell of the Poor Law legacy and the socially divisive attitudes and practices which stemmed from it.'

It is likely that such a philosophy is shared by the majority of the senior officials who read this book as well as by large numbers of their committee members and large numbers of their staffs. Nevertheless, it will need to be proclaimed, implicitly and explicitly, to diverse groups of people with very different backgrounds of experience and very different attitudes. If the new service is to be imbued with this philosophy considerable changes in orientation, in this deeper and more radical meaning of the phrase, will have to take place and there may well be some problems ahead of Directors in persuading all their grass-roots social workers and residential workers and day-centre staffs (and perhaps some committee members too) that they should embrace it. Directors and senior staff and training officers will need to help people to discard outworn methods of looking at social diagnosis and treatment-selection in the individual, symptom-centred, blinkered way which has been a feature of some of our social services, and to replace this outlook with a dynamic, family-orientated, situational one. They will need to imbue all concerned with a spirit of enthusiasm and the notion of promoting social health rather than merely ameliorating social disease; moving away from the strait-jacket of a crisis-centred approach toward the planned deployment of resources in a positive, educative and preventive programme which is not merely 'integrated', but also, to use a word which has gone out of fashion, 'dedicated'.

Change of organisational size

Our final type of change was *change of organisational size.* It will be remembered that one of the arguments mentioned by the Seebohm Committee as having been levelled in evidence against the notion of integrated social service departments was that they would be 'too big for humanity or efficiency and lose the "personal touch" '. In paragraph 159 of its

Report the Committee said that it did not believe 'there is any ground for fear on this score' and went on to deal with the argument on the ground of efficiency. The problem of 'humanity' and the 'personal touch' then somehow got forgotten and was not alluded to again in the Report. This may be thought to be unfortunate, for although increased size is not a strong argument against the setting-up of unified departments, it is an argument against forgetting all about the human problems that are involved when one increases the size of the work-organisation beyond a certain point. For this reason it will be incumbent upon Directors and their Committees to pay a great deal of attention to the need for 'humanising' the organisation both for clients and for staff. This will involve a whole range of measures from the introduction of good reception and referral procedures to the provision of comfortable and well-furnished waiting rooms, and will include some thought being given to the designing of easily-understood notices and forms and the couching of letters in English rather than in pompous local authority 'gobbledegook'.

It is important to recognise, of course, that many of the changes we have discussed also have a positive aspect. Staff may be able to see in the various changes in which they are caught up a better career structure; a greater likelihood of skilled supervision becoming available; opportunities for more training; the acquisition of higher status; the availability of increased and improved resources; the provision of better working conditions; the opportunities to do better, more effective, perhaps more worthwhile work; more clearly formulated and articulated agency policies; greater professional direction from the top; and the feeling that they are sharing in and contributing to an exciting new venture in social service provision which will be looked back upon in years to come as an historic turning-point.

Perhaps it is in these positive aspects of change (and there may be others which are important subjectively to some individuals) that one may discern the opportunities for dealing with some of the negative, and in our view the one we mentioned last – the feeling that one is sharing in and contributing to something which is worthwhile and exciting – is the most important of all of them. 'Sharing in and contributing to', although we have bracketed them together, really need considering separately. 'Sharing in' means not only sharing the load, playing one's part, doing one's bit; it also means being trusted, knowing what is going on, playing a part in the decision-making. We have already suggested that one powerful component in the generation of anxiety about change is ignorance – ignorance of what is going on, ignorance of what may be going to happen in the future. Fear of the unknown is a powerful emotion in us all and one that is easily triggered. Nature abhors a vacuum and in the absence of reliable information concerning those matters which are important to us, unreliable information (rumour) can spread very rapidly.

Good communication, therefore, is vital from the very beginning. Communication, if it is to be effective, must be unequivocal. Not only is ambiguity in communication a cause of rumour, but it needs also to be remembered that the recipient of information, if it is not crystal clear, is likely to restructure it according to his own point of view and to suit his own wishes. But let us add the other factor – a sense of 'contributing to'. Good communication is not only unambiguous, it is not one-way either. It is not merely a passing of information (or instructions) down the line. Effective communication, particularly in an organisation in which there are large numbers of professional staff, involves *dialogue,* involves *interaction,* involves *participation.* Individuals who find themselves in the uncertain situation that has been described will need to feel that they have a contribution to make, that the skills and knowledge and experience they possess have value and are seen to have value. But it is more than this. We are not so much concerned with what is 'therapeutic' for staff as with what is necessary for the organisation, and we must not be so beguiled by all our pyramid-shaped charts that we make the false assumption that all wisdom resides at the apex. Communication upward is not just valuable for those below who are originating the message – it is essential for those above who are receiving it, for not only are they likely themselves to have areas of ignorance crying out to be filled, but unless they know what is being said and thought and felt by subordinates, they cannot themselves function effectively.

Space does not permit a full discussion of the mechanisms through which effective communication within the department can be mediated, though in different ways there is some discussion of them in Chapters 3 and 5. They are likely to be both of a formal and an informal kind and include such things as staff meetings, group seminars, news-sheets, bulletins, staff magazines, in-service training schemes, individual supervision and consultation, day conferences, library facilities, working parties, innovation groups, and so on.

Some of these mechanisms may seem to have uses other than as vehicles for communication, but we need to remind ourselves that what is being discussed here is not only the communication of *information,* but also the mutual interchange of ideas, feelings and attitudes. Algie, in an important article in the *British Hospital Journal* (351) has borrowed the notion of the 'sentient group' from Miller and Rice (230) and the phrase almost exactly connotes what we have in mind, though, in our view, such groups should be instrumental rather than merely self-fulfilling and they would not provide the *only* means by which professional and individual expression of ideas and feelings can be provided either.

F.C. Mann (382) points to a number of related sets of facts which make for the efficacy of systematic feedback of information through 'organisational families':

1. participation in the interpretation and analysis of research findings leads to the internalisation of information and beliefs. When ideas are a person's own they are much more likely to be translated into meaningful practices than when they are the suggestions of an outsider;
2. the feedback of information and its discussion by the appropriate organisational family makes it highly relevant to the functioning of the sub-group and its members. Principles taught at a general level of abstraction are more difficult to apply than the discovery of principles from a person's own immediate experience;
3. knowledge of results can in itself motivate people toward improving their performance;
4. group support is especially effective where there is continuing membership in a particular group.

We feel sure that there are many other advantages to be derived from this kind of activity. For example, depending on the quality of the leadership, it may be possible to introduce some of the ideas which have been pioneered in this country by the Tavistock Institute and discussed in books like Jaques' *The Changing Culture of a Factory* (202). Jaques and his associates take the view that social systems function as a means of defence against anxiety. (Some readers may recall a demonstration of this kind in the nursing profession (334).) It therefore follows that changes in the system will be resisted because they threaten such defences. There has not been opportunity in this Chapter to spell out in any detail the concept of resistance to change, though in everything that has been said this notion has been implicit. The manner in which resistance manifests itself in particular individuals or particular groups can, of course, vary enormously, and, as with the ego-defences associated with the name of Anna Freud (173), some of these resistances are conscious, others unconscious. To quote from Jaques (202):

'The process of helping a group to unearth and identify some of the less obvious influences affecting its behavious is one borrowed from medical psycho-therapy, from which is borrowed also the technical term *working through*. It presupposes access by a consultant trained in group methods to a group accepting the task of examining its own behaviour as and while it occurs, and a group able to learn, with the aid of interpretive comment, to recognise an increasing number of forces, both internal and external, that are influencing its behaviour. The expectation, then, is that the group will acquire a better capacity to tolerate initially independent insights into phenomena such as scape-goating, rivalry, dependency, jealousy, futility and despair and thence a greater ability to deal effectively with difficulty reality problems. When we speak of a group working through a problem we mean considerably more than is ordinarily meant by saying that a full discussion of a problem has taken place. We mean that a serious attempt has been made to voice the unrecognised difficulties, often socially taboo, which have been preventing it from going ahead with whatever task it may have had.'

But aside from such sophisticated concepts, on the merely common-sense level it seem fairly obvious that the kind of changes in 'orientation' that are going to be necessary to the formation and effective functioning of the new departments are unlikely to be achieved by any individual in isolation from his professional colleagues, nor are they likely to be assimilated simply because of a change in assigned role. A simple concept in psychology is that of *perseveration* – the tendency to carry on with the same activity. This can be extended to mean going on doing the same things in the way we have always done them, and the difficulty people experience in switching from one activity (or method of performing it) to another. Sometimes this tendency to *perseverate* arises from inertia. Inertia does not, as we might suppose, connote lack of activity (though the word 'inert' might lead us to think it does) but lack of change in activity; that is to say, the property of a body to continue in its existing state of uniform motion in a straight line unless that state is changed by an external force. With human beings, however, we have to be careful about the kind of external force we apply and the way in which we apply it, if we are successfully to bring about change. Sometimes our intervention can have the effect of reinforcing the subject's determination to 'carry on regardless'; indeed it is likely to do so if the person applying the external force (or influence) is not seen as understanding the difficulties which the subject experiences in achieving the desired change.

Working together in 'multi-disciplinary' teams (i.e. teams comprised of persons coming from a variety of specialisms in social work (and we should not forget the residential and day-centre workers in this context) should be an educative experience, in the widest sense, for all concerned, provided there is some readiness to learn from each other and to share new attitudes rather than to cling determinedly to what used to be. We need to recognise, however, that the mixing together of heterogeneous individuals will not, of itself, produce concensus, and active steps will have to be taken to prevent friction and conflict arising, for example from the attempt by some to impose old patterns of working on the whole group, or from the need in others to displace their loyalty outside the group.

Making the unfamiliar familiar will be something of a struggle for all concerned, and it will be important to remember that although the promulgation of clear directives concerning the delegation of responsibilities and the wide and unambiguous dissemination of policy decisions will be extremely important, it will also be necessary to build into the system opportunities for all personnel to discuss their individual difficulties with a sympathetic and understanding individual supervisor. The skills of supervision in social work agencies in this country are now beginning to be recognised as an essential ingredient of agency practice. In a time of change such as is ahead of us, they will be required more than ever, and it will be for Directors to place high priority on the equipping of their 'middle-management' to develop and practise them.

The psychological problems with which this chapter has been concerned are, of course, only a small part of the large overall problem that will face Directors in the new departments, but they are an important part. Change, as we have tried to argue, can trigger off all kinds of chain reactions. It can result in alterations to the power and prestige structure (which is bound to be to *someone's* disadvantage); it can test the degree of commitment of all staff very severely; it can impel people to utilise all manner of irrational defences, from hyperactive but essentially goalless behaviour at one end of the scale to withdrawal into apathetic inactivity at the other. It can impel us all to examine afresh what our goals are – indeed to ask ourselves the fundamental question: 'What do we mean by goals?' and we are reminded, in this connection, of the example of the group of bricklayers who when asked what they were doing could equally well have answered 'We're laying bricks', 'We're building a wall' or 'We're helping to build a cathedral'!

Of course, the unconscious mind has a part to play too in this question of goals, and as Rice (272) pointed out, there is sometimes an unconscious re-definition of the primary task as the preservation of the institution for its own sake. Institutions, particularly, seem to have the power to 'take over' the people who ostensibly run them, and the institution becomes the end to be served, rather than the means by which some other (human) end is secured. This may be something we shall all need to watch very carefully when we come to think about the future role of the various Community Homes that are to emerge, like fabulous birds, from the ashes of the old.

In the next two Chapters both the problem of the shape of the new departments and the problem of deciding on a rational series of steps to be taken within a pre-determined time span are discussed. This concept of Time was discussed most usefully by Ginsberg and Reilley in a paper entitled 'The Process of Change' (in 220) and in borrowing from them we may, for our purposes, list the stages of such a process-through-time as being roughly:

27

1. finding appropriate methods of analysing the situation;
2. developing the plan (and this will include the participation of the staff, as we have indicated above);
3. deciding to accept the plan;
4. announcing the plan to the organisation;
5. detailing new functions and responsibilities;
6. aligning and harmonising the various operational systems to support the implementation of the plan;
7. active instruction of key personnel;
8. implementing the plan;
9. adjusting the plan in the light of experience.

Setting out the stages in this way (and each one may have many sub-items) underlines the fact that Change of the kind we are considering, is not so much an Event as a Process, a process which exists in time. Psychologically, as well as operationally, time is important in our planning. There has to be time for communication systems to get working, time for anxieties to become controlled, time for new skills to be acquired, and so on – and we shall ignore this very important factor at our peril. It may, however, be the case that the *length* of time is less important than the way in which we fill it and there is some evidence to suggest that the process of integration may take a somewhat shorter length of time to achieve than is sometimes supposed. This is not a matter on which we can make a recommendation which would be of universal application and the specimen time-chart in Chapter 4 is not intended to be definitive.

Qualities of leadership in the Director of the new Department will, of course, be of paramount importance, for the harmonising of the activities of a group of people with widely differing backgrounds will demand that he secures their real co-operation and active and enthusiastic participation in 'working for change'. That there will be some resistance is, as we have indicated, incvitable, and Directors must expect a certain amount of hostility and blame. They will be expected to be both demons and supermen (or women) and blamed because they are human. But if they can provide the kind of leadership which enables all staff truly to feel they are 'helping to build a cathedral' most of the mistakes they are bound to make are likely to be forgiven them.

3. The Structure and Organisation of the New Department

REFERENCE was made in Chapter 1 to the need for the structure of a social service organisation to develop through several stages, ranging from the recognition of the existence of particular human needs to the formulation of overall objectives and the development of procedures for the giving, the reviewing and the evaluating of services to meet those needs.

The Director of the new unified department, however, will not be starting with a clean sheet, but taking over all, or parts of, three already functioning departments, each with a long list of statutory and other responsibilities. Because of the fragmented nature of the former services, it is unlikely that the human needs for which the new department will have to assume some responsibility will have been investigated in any *comprehensive* way; neither will the combined knowledge available within the component parts of the department (i.e. the 'constituent departments') serve as an adequate substitute for this. At the same time, it is likely that all the resources that are initially available in terms of staff, finance and capital goods will be found to be already stretched to their limits in meeting the more obvious human needs that will have been already recognised. It is possible, as the Seebohm Committee suggested, that a more rational re-organisation and re-deployment of existing resources can lead to some economies, but these are likely to be more than compensated for by the discovery of (and the assumption of responsibility for meeting) many more hitherto unrecognised and unmet needs, so there are likely to be considerable pressures on local authorities for the provision of considerably increased resources, despite the chill statement in the Local Authority Social Services Bill that 'The Bill is therefore not expected to result in any significant increase in expenditure out of public funds . . . (nor) . . . any appreciable overall effects on public service manpower requirements'.

Some Directors are already facing the dilemma whether, in planning the organisational structure of their new Department, they should have regard to present or future needs. It is likely that, in the event, it will simply not be possible to delay taking basic decisions. Local authority social services staff have been facing great uncertainties for a long time and it will be important, in introducing structural change, that it should not continue to be tentative, provisional, and ambiguous but provide some stability and certainty. This will be necessary not only to the resolution of staff uncertainty and anxiety, already discussed in the previous chapter, but also in maintaining service at a high level during the period of transition.

It is true, of course, that unless a degree of flexibility is built into the new organisational structure it is difficult later to introduce further major changes, but although as time goes on and more knowledge is gained and hitherto unrecognised needs come to light, it is unlikely that these would require major alteration to the *structure*. Since the publication of the Seebohm Committee Report and particularly since the publication of the Local Authority Social Services Bill a number of organisational 'models' have been put forward in journal articles and many of these have stressed the need for a structure geared to active community participation and staff-involvement in problem solving. Some models have superimposed 'sentient-group', special-interest group and working-party sub-systems on top of the hierarchical delegation system, and inasmuch as a 'polyarchic' model of this kind serves to demonstrate the importance of lateral communication, of shared activity at all levels in thinking about a multiplicity of problems and of tapping-in to areas of specialist expertise for professional advice, it can be extremely useful. Many who have studied such models, however, must have felt them to be unduly complicated, blurring as they do the essential distinction between a communications network which is delegatory and characterised by a principle of 'accountability', and a communications network which is essentially designed for advisory, consultative or 'staff development' purposes. That both sets of relationships may be necessary is not in doubt, but to attempt to combine them in one organisational chart can result in confusion rather than clarification.

Barbara Butler has somewhere written that 'the Seebohm plan seems to require a bureaucratic structure containing organic modules ... Both area office teams and residential establishments would seem to function most effectively on the organic model, but each needs a hierarchical structure as a containing framework'. For some people, the term 'bureaucratic' has a highly pejorative flavour, conjuring up images of a large-scale organisation dedicated to the pursuit of a ruthless efficiency acquired at the expense of humanity and requiring of its servants a docile and unquestioning conformity to a rigid set of rules. This is, of course, a fantasy. The bureaucratic structure outlined in Figure 2 is intended as a diagrammatic representation of certain lines of communication within an organisation. It cannot pretend to describe *all* the lines of communication which will exist within any real organisation, nor can it prescribe the manner or spirit in which particular communications, upward or downward, are couched. Servility and authoritarianism are not so much the outcomes of an organisation's shape as of the personalities of those who fill the roles within it. Chapter 2 has already emphasised the importance placed by the authors on the fostering of opportunities for all staff to 'share in' and 'contribute to' the work of the whole department by developing both formal and informal machinery of all kinds which may promote this. This in no way affects the argument that, for *certain* purposes, namely the delegation of tasks, the division of responsibilities, the building-in of 'accountability', the issuing of instructions 'down the line' and the passing of reports 'upward', the bureaucratic model is the recommended model. For the kind of purposes mentioned, it is the best possible model, since it is efficient and clearly unambiguous. Whether the particular form of the bureaucratic model outlined in Figure 2 is the best will depend upon a number of factors, some of them having to do with local conditions, some with considerations of size, some with the availability of actual members of staff to fill particular roles, but the authors have little doubt that a basically bureaucratic structure as a 'containing framework for organic modules' is likely, in some form or other, to be adopted by most if not all social services authorities.

It is likely, of course, that as the new organisation gets under way and begins to accumulate more and more knowledge concerning the area for which it has responsibility, it will have to revise its original ideas concerning priorities and the relative proportions of available resources which should be allocated in particular directions. Such re-appraisal of policies, however, should not affect basic structures. A structure broadly similar to the one suggested in this Chapter, though doubtless differing in details, is likely to be necessary because in any social services department that can be envisaged many people will be involved in meeting the overall objectives of the agency and it will be essential that their differing roles and functions be co-ordinated into a unified whole. A basic premise of the bureaucratic model is that every position in the structure should have its functions clearly defined so that the person allocated to each position knows what is expected of him and knows that he has been given the authority necessary to the performance of his functions. It does not mean, however, that, outside the formal hierarchical structure, a person occupying a position within it may not have other roles (as the leader, perhaps, of a working party set up to study a particular aspect of the agency's activities, or as a specialist consultant). Within the formal hierarchical structure, however, there will be clearly laid down lines of communication and accountability.

From this it follows that the Director, who is ultimately responsible to the Social Services Committee for the work of the Department (though having other roles to carry as well – for example in relation to the Chief Officers' Team) must delegate sufficient authority to every person under his jurisdiction in order to ensure that, for each position, the responsibility is matched by the necessary amount of authority over resources (including staff resources) to enable the responsibilities to be met. It can only be where responsibility and authority are matched in this way that individual accountability can be accepted as just and reasonable.

Bureaucracy has often been associated with one-way communication, with the assumption that the higher echelons possess the knowledge and wisdom necessary to the formulation of policy and the giving of directions, while the roles of the lower echelons require nothing more of the personnel filling them than that they do what they are told. The findings of empirical studies which have sought to determine the types of formal authority which are conducive to greatest production effort are inconclusive, even contradictory and thus provide no reliable guide for determining the optimum allocation of authority and responsibility. The nature of much social service provision however suggests that first-line social workers require a considerable amount of authority and autonomy in determining how they should work with their clients and that their role boundaries should be quite broad. It would be appropriate, for example, to hold them accountable for how they handle a caseload but not accountable for how they spend a particular working day. It should be recognised too, that it is the first-line or face-to-face worker who should know how the service given is perceived by its recipients, where improvement is required and where gaps in service exist. Workers at all levels should be encouraged to communicate their knowledge, their ideas and their reactions to proposed policies and procedures and the organisation should be so structured as to ensure this up-flowing of communication. This can be achieved in a variety of ways, including meetings of residential staffs, by area teams meeting together at regular intervals to examine and discuss their functions, their clients and the services they give; and through working parties set up to investigate and discuss matters of specific interest. As such groups would not have executive powers but would be advisory in nature, the positions within them would not need to follow the bureaucratic hierarchical pattern; it might, for example, be appropriate for a basic grade social worker to chair such a group while an Assistant Director of Social Services filled a position of ordinary member.

In brief, upward communication will normally take the form of information and advice while downward communication is likely to be in the form of direction, dissemination of information and the provision of guide-lines. A recipient of a directive needs to be clear what is expected of him and while orders may sometimes incur some resentment, uncertainty usually incurs more. Instructions should not be so cosily couched as to raise doubts as to whether they are orders or not. Equally, only the minimum number of orders should be communicated as is sufficient to ensure that departmental requirements are met. They should be well thought out, have their purpose explained, and, if likely to arouse controversy,

FIGURE 2

A SUGGESTED ORGANISATIONAL STRUCTURE OF
A LOCAL AUTHORITY SOCIAL SERVICES DEPARTMENT

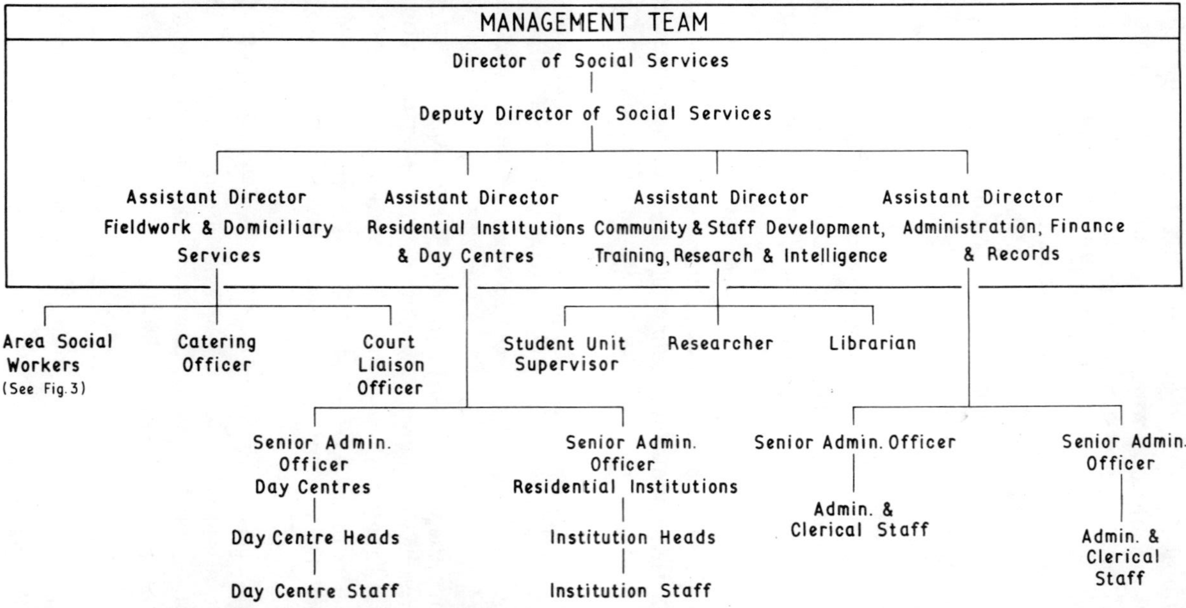

MANAGEMENT TEAM

Director of Social Services

Deputy Director of Social Services

Assistant Director
Fieldwork & Domiciliary Services

Assistant Director
Residential Institutions & Day Centres

Assistant Director
Community & Staff Development, Training, Research & Intelligence

Assistant Director
Administration, Finance & Records

Catering Officer

Court Liaison Officer

Student Unit Supervisor

Researcher

Librarian

Senior Admin. Officer

Senior Admin. Officer

Area Social Workers
(See Fig.3)

Senior Admin. Officer
Day Centres

Senior Admin. Officer
Residential Institutions

Admin. & Clerical Staff

Admin. & Clerical Staff

Day Centre Heads

Institution Heads

Day Centre Staff

Institution Staff

NB. Specialist consultant functions can additionally be allotted where appropriate.

they might perhaps be presented first in draft form for discussion and reaction. Once officially promulgated, however, they should not be changed or amended too readily. The department needs to know where it is going and how it is getting there and the nature and frequency of directive should reflect this.

The headquarters of the department will be responsible for ensuring that the statutory and other requirements laid upon the department are fully met. It will need to be sufficiently removed from the hurly-burly of day-to-day activity to be able to acquire new knowledge, to deliberate and plan in a quiet atmosphere, yet at the same time remain sensitive to the changing needs of the community, the clientele and the department's staff. The management team will need to know as far as can reasonably be ascertained, the nature and extent of the social problems of the district; to develop the department's philosophy in relation to these problems; to define its overall objectives; to formulate overall policies; to develop programmes and procedures; and through the recruitment, training and deployment of staff, ensure that these programmes and procedures are carried out. At the same time, it will need continually to evaluate all its policies and practices in order to become more efficient and effective and to remain sensitive and responsive to changing needs; and to equip itself to provide and plan well for the future.

With these objectives in mind, a suggested organisational model is presented in Figure 2.

It will be noted that this model provides for both a Director and a Deputy Director. This is at variance with a number of other recently presented models which appear to be based on the assumption that it is the function of the Director to co-ordinate the work of the Assistant Directors and that a Deputy merely means an additional (and an unnecessary) link in the authority chain. For the purpose of determining whether or not the establishment should include a Deputy Director the functions that might be allocated to a Director and a Deputy Director need to be examined.

The Director

Outside the Social Services Committee itself, the ultimate responsibility for determining the work that is to be performed by the department and the responsibility for the type and quality of the work that is currently being carried out, must rest with the Director, who is the Committee's executive officer. It will be necessary for him to ensure that sufficient information is forthcoming from the department and the balancing of authority and responsibility, that an implemented and that the necessary resources are calculated, sought, and obtained and that they are utilised in such a way, through a rational division of labour, allocation of functions and the balancing of authority and responsibility that an adequate job performance is achieved by all staff in the department. It will be his function to approve draft policy documents prior to their submission to the Committee; to meet regularly with members of the Social Services Committee; to liaise with community and other agencies, and to be responsible for high level public relations. The department will be the main instrument of social services development in the district but it will not be the only one, and it will be essential that its Director should be available to meet people who might be influential in this work. While he is likely to possess greater authority and carry more responsibility than other social work agency heads in his district they will quite properly expect to be able to communicate direct with him – as one agency head to another – and time must be made available for these contacts.

The Director will need to be freed from supervising or participating in the day-to-day work of the separate sectors of the headquarters staff and to spend a great deal of time in forward planning and in getting out and meeting people. In line with the development of corporate management within local authorities following the publication of the Maud Committee Report it is to be expected that the Director of Social Services will become a member of the Chief Officers' Team. Although such membership will inevitably emphasise the new status that has been achieved by social work and personal social service within local authorities, this is not the reason for it. The Director will have a contribution to make to the work of the Chief Officers' Team. He is likely to be in possession of information within his Department that is not available elsewhere in the authority, information which can make an important contribution to overall planning. His professional concern with people and their personal and social problems will enable him to provide a perspective which will almost certainly be of value to his chief officer colleagues. But in underlining this, it is important that we should not forget that his membership of the team will also enable him to learn a great deal, not only in terms of the acquisition of information otherwise not available to his department, but also in terms of acquiring a wider understanding of the work of his department within the broad context of local government activity as a whole. His membership is also likely to provide him with some much needed support and encouragement from colleagues who will be much more experienced than he in the carrying of heavy departmental responsibilities.

Of all his functions, however, it is probably the function of *leader* which is the most important. A large, newly formed department struggling to achieve a corporate identity is going to need leadership of high quality – charismatic leadership no less than professional leadership. This cannot be provided if the Director remains imprisoned in his office, buried under piles of files and concerning himself with the minutiae of departmental activity. In all but the smallest departments, therefore, there is a strong case for the appointment of a Deputy Director.

The Deputy Director

The establishment of a Deputy Director of Social Services should not present any difficulties for sizeable local authorities since it is likely that precedents for the appointment of Deputies in other major departments will already exist. In a department as large and complex as the social services department is likely to be, the argument for such an appointment is an overwhelming one. As Figure 2 makes clear, it is envisaged that instead of dividing functions (as at present) between Child Care, Welfare Services and Mental Health, it will make for greater integration and rationalisation to divide them between field work, domiciliary services, residential and day care services, and community and staff development, each sector being headed by an Assistant Director, with an additional Assistant Director in charge of administrative services. A quadripartite arrangement of this kind renders the establishment of a position between the Director and the Assistant Directors highly desirable, providing someone who can on the one hand exercise a more intimate, day-to-day

37

oversight of departmental activities as a whole than is possible for the Director himself to assume, and on the other hand deputise for the Director when for any reason he is away from the Department, without upsetting the balance between the Assistant Directorships.

The Assistant Director for Fieldwork and Domiciliary Services

This Assistant Director would, as his title implies and as is shown in Figure 2, be directly responsible to the Deputy Director (although ultimately to the Director) for the work of the Area Social Workers and their teams (see Figure 3). He might also, where considered appropriate, have directly under his control a catering officer carrying responsibility for meals on wheels and other similar services, though it may be that in some areas there might be good reasons for establishing such a post under the direction of the Assistant Director for Residential Institutions and Day Centres. Also under the direction of the Assistant Director for Fieldwork and Domiciliary Services would be the court liaison officer (possibly with a team of assistants) who would represent the department in the courts and liaise directly with area social workers and institution heads concerning reports for the courts and feeding back information concerning court disposals.

The Assistant Director for Fieldwork and Domiciliary Services will need, both under the direction of the Director and Deputy Director, and otherwise, to work in close co-operation with his Assistant Director colleagues. Some services that he will wish to develop will clearly come under his exclusive direction, others can only be provided in conjunction with other sectors. For example, lunch club facilities and laundry facilities might need to be provided in co-operation with the Residential and Day Centre sector, gardening services, simple visiting and so on, in co-operation with the community development sector, though in this latter connection it will be noted that in Figure 3 it is envisaged that voluntary workers will be allocated to area teams.

The Assistant Director's main function, however, will be to take responsibility for the development of high-quality fieldwork and domiciliary services and for co-ordinating the work of the Area Social Workers and their teams. His work will involve on the one hand active membership of the department's 'management team' and on the other regular contact with Area Social Workers. These area contacts will be especially important and in this connection the Assistant Director will need to concern himself with providing the essential link between the 'areas' and headquarters; assisting the areas to develop in their own ways but communicating and interpreting the broad departmental policies within which such area development may take place. Initially, as the 'shape' of the new department begins to form he will doubtless need to be closely concerned not only with 'policy' but also with the development and implementation of 'procedures' (in the building up of area teams and the assigning of cases to them, for example, and for assisting in the designing of 'intake procedures', agency 'forms' and agreed 'methods of working').

The Assistant Director for Residential Institutions and Day Centres

The Assistant Director responsible for residential institutions and day centres, is likely to require two main 'arms' each under a senior administrative officer, responsible respectively for the work of day centres and of residential establishments. The siting of day centres and residential institutions by a local authority may or may not reflect the current needs of the immediate neighbourhood in which they stand, but overall it is unlikely, that the distribution of all establishments within a local authority's boundaries will 'mesh in' with the geographical location of area teams. Inevitably, one area team will have an excessive number of centres and institutions in its area, and others an insufficiency. As a general rule therefore it will be appropriate to rationalise the organisation of day centres and institutions within the headquarters team and not on an area basis. Such an arrangement allows area teams, while making their needs known in relation to day centre and residential resources, to concentrate on the provision of field work and domiciliary services, although, as has been said, maintaining close contact with day centres and institutions.

As the concept of the 'community home' develops and the large-scale re-organisation of local authority personal social service gets under way, it is likely that residential provision of all kinds will be increasingly reviewed, re-appraised and rationalised. In many sectors a wide gap has been allowed to develop between 'fieldwork' and 'residential work', a gap affecting adequate communication and co-operation between the two and therefore contributing to or perpetuating differences in professional philosophies, ideologies, attitudes and practices as well as differences in status, degree of professionalism, working conditions, salaries and promotion prospects. The unifying of local authority personal social services will hopefully provide the opportunity, the incentive and the means to improve this lamentable situation. Such a re-appraisal will need to be undertaken at all levels, both within the Headquarters team and within and between the residential establishments themselves.

Inasmuch as residential establishments of different kinds will have grown up under quite separate administrations, the placing of all of them, irrespective of specialist function, under one Assistant Director (and with them the day centres too) will have considerable implications for their future development, for their optimum utilisation, and for their relationship with each other and with the 'field'. The task of promoting this aspect of 'integration' will primarily fall to the Assistant Director of this sector and he and his staff at headquarters will need to acquire, quite rapidly, a realistic picture of the overall situation, to establish good working relations with the establishments themselves and in consultation with them to develop draft policies and procedures for consideration by the management team and onward transmission through the Director to the Social Services Committee. To this sector of the organisation will fall a very wide range of duties, including the devising of appropriate admission criteria, the inspection of and maintenance of standards within establishments, the planning of new establishments, the adaptation of existing ones, the furnishing and maintenance of buildings of all kinds, and, in collaboration with the Assistant Director concerned with staff development, enabling all staff to acquire the skills, expertise and understanding which will permit the regimes within the establishments to be geared more and more appropriately to meet inmate need.

The oversight and development of day centre provision will also be an important function and in some ways perhaps more difficult since many establishments of this kind will be initially geared to a medically-orientated administration and their personnel less closely identified with a specifically 'social work' ideology. If this is the case, it will be all the more important that strenuous efforts be made to avoid day centre staffs harbouring the idea that they are in some way peripheral to the main concerns of the organisation as a whole and to 'integrate' them fully in the activities of the Department. This task can be undertaken in a variety of ways – through in-service training, through their membership of multi-disciplinary working parties, through their participation in case conferences, and so on, but a great deal will also depend upon the attention the Assistant Director gives to each Day Centre, since he above all is likely to be perceived as the 'persona' of the new Department.

The Assistant Director for Community and Staff Development, Training, Research and Intelligence

This sector of the headquarters organisation will be an extremely important one – indeed in some of the larger authorities it might be necessary to divide its functions under two separate Assistant Directors. In most departments, however, it is likely that one Assistant Director will be able to assume responsibility for all the activities implied in the title, though it is crucial that great care be taken in the appointment of the right man or woman for this onerous job. The Seebohm Committee report rightly emphasises the need for much more to be done than has been achieved hitherto in developing community participation in the meeting of individual and family needs. Close liaison with voluntary organisations of all kinds at both national and local level will need to be established and maintained, considerable assistance may have to be made available to many groups in the local community as well as in eliciting help from them, and in fostering a working partnership between the Department and community groups and organisations it is likely that a basis will be laid for future developments in a number of different directions. In addition to this, there is no doubt that a considerable amount of goodwill and desire to help exist in the community which so far have been untapped and unexploited. It is envisaged that the appointment of an Assistant Director who has special responsibility in this area of activity may do much to mobilise it and give it shape and direction. The Assistant Director will not, therefore, concern himself only with bodies of people who are already organised in some way, but also with discovering, recruiting, training (or preparing) and making

41

available to the department suitable individual *volunteers* (247).

In addition to this responsibility, the Assistant Director would be responsible for Staff Development and for the co-ordination of training within the Department. Staff development (or in-service training) will be one of the key activities of the whole department and in some way or other an activity which is likely to involve all members of staff. It deserves a chapter to itself and is, therefore, discussed in Chapter 5. The co-ordination of training, however, will involve not only the planning, oversight and integration of in-service training schemes, but also accepting administrative responsibility for the co-ordination and oversight of those members of staff who may be concerned in the field training or residential training of students from bona fide professional courses of various kinds.

As is argued in Chapter 6, it will be important both for the healthy development of social service departments as well as their optimum effectiveness that more systematic attention is given to the question of agency-based on-going research into the agency's activities. Much information is already collected and stored by social work agencies, though it would seem that little of it is ever *used;* much vital information is also lacking simply because it has never been collected. If the new departments are to reverse this state of affairs they may find it necessary to set up a small research and intelligence section *within the department.* If this is to be done it may be appropriate to allocate the administrative responsibility for it to the same Assistant Director as takes responsibility for training and staff development matters. Such a unit, which might need to include one or more research officers, research assistants and a librarian, would be independent of any larger research unit set up in the local authority as a whole, though it would work in close collaboration with it and need to share perhaps its computer and other resources.

The Assistant Director for Administration, Finance and Records

Though this position in the organisation need not be filled by a professionally trained social worker, it is desirable that the person appointed to this Assistant Directorship should be not only highly experienced and skilled in the handling of the administrative and fiscal matters with which he will be concerned but also sympathetic toward social welfare and the overall aims of the department. As Figure 2 indicates, it is envisaged that he may need two (or more) senior administrative officers working under his supervision, each responsible for a team of administrative and clerical workers.

The Management Team

The structure thus far described (and as shown in Figure 2) is one which enables the Director, his Deputy and four Assistant Directors to comprise a small, but highly effective, Management Team. The team would doubtless meet together regularly (possibly daily) to discuss, to plan and to co-ordinate the work of the Department as a whole. The precise ways in which such a team would decide to work cannot be generally prescribed, it will be for each Management Team to work out its own methods for itself. It will be important, however, that it should, from the outset, be clear about which responsibilities are carried by which officer and *to whom* each officer is accountable. (For example, does membership of a Management Team imply that, in addition to a particular Assistant Director's accountability to the Director, he is also in some sense accountable to his colleagues in the team? Does the discussion by the team of matters pertaining to his particular sector of responsibility imply a right not only to receive information but also to issue directives? Is the team a 'talking shop' or an executive body?) The authors of this book make no recommendations in this regard beyond stressing the need, when setting up a structure, to ensure that everyone within the structure is clear about the nature and purpose of that structure and about his own roles within it.

It may be added, however, that, of itself, structure cannot achieve anything, it can only make achievement possible or impossible, can only enable or disable, can only provide channels through which action can flow. A good structure will assist the achievement of ends – the channels will be of the requisite width and depth and point in the right directions – but however good it is, the structure cannot guarantee results – these will depend upon people, upon attitudes and upon resources.

The Area Teams

The plan set out in Figure 2 makes the Assistant Director

for Fieldwork and Domiciliary Services responsible for controlling or supervising a number of Area Social Workers, each of whom will be responsible for an Area Team comprising a number of smaller units. It is these units who (like the day-centre and residential staff) will in the main be the actual givers of service. Whereas the purpose of the Headquarters structure described above is to ensure that this service is appropriate, is of good quality and is efficient (a purpose which will be pursued by providing the support needed by the first-line workers) it is likely to be the case that to the majority of clients it will be the first-line worker who 'is' the department. In one sense the unified service has consumed its competitors and become something of a monopoly, and to the extent that this is true a greater responsibility is thereby placed upon it to ensure that it truly meets client need and meets it with compassion and due regard for human dignity.

The Area Teams, if they are to fulfil their appropriate functions and meet the expectations that will be made of them, need to be:

    (a)   community-based;

    (b)   client- and family-centred;

    (c)   accessible;

    (d)   efficient;

    (e)   effective; and, so far as fieldwork and domicilary services are concerned,

    (f)   comprehensive.

Each Area Social Worker (and his team) should be allocated to a suitably-sized geographical area for which he will be responsible. The siting of the Area office may be very important. If possible, it should be in a central location within an area of service, but a number of factors will affect the decision about this, including the availability of suitable accommodation and the transport facilities in the area. (In some cities, for example, it is easier for people to travel from the outskirts to the city centre than to travel laterally across the city.) (See also (373).) For some Departments it may well be the case that small 'neighbourhood units' should additionally be sited on certain housing estates, or 'advice centres' or 'shops' provided to meet the immediate needs of particular neighbourhoods, as suggested in paragraph 593 of the Seebohm Committee Report.

Unless Areas are very large, it is unlikely that it will be

necessary (except for neighbourhood units) to sub-divide further on a geographical basis; indeed it may be important that all team members should be concerned for the whole area for which the team has responsibility. It is highly probable, however, that the size of these teams will need to be rather larger than the 10 to 12 social worker size referred to in the Seebohm Committee Report and it is important to remember that the Committee did not regard these numbers as optima. A possible model of an Area Team is presented in Figure 3.

It is desirable that each Area Team should carry as much responsibility for its own functioning as is possible and that, within the limits of the overall philosophy, policies and departmental procedures of the organisation as a whole, the maximum degree of autonomy should be delegated to each Area Social Worker. Indeed this was recommended in paragraph 592 of the Seebohm Committee Report.

As Figure 3 makes clear, it is envisaged that a typical Area Team might consist of two or more 'general casework units', a specialist unit, and an 'intensive casework unit'. These units would be 'serviced' by one or more home help units, a community development unit (which will include a number of 'volunteers') and a finance and administration unit. As with the role positions in the Headquarters structure, specialist consultant functions can be additionally attached to any persons within the structure who may have specialist expertise which might be valuable to members of the Team.

The reason for including a specialist services unit is that it is envisaged that certain groups of clients (e.g. the physically handicapped, the blind and the deaf) may require of the social workers who are in touch with them (and with their families) a degree of specialist knowledge unlikely to be possessed or quickly acquired by general social workers (knowledge of Braille or Moon, for example). It may be unnecessary to allocate such workers to a specialist unit, of course; attachment of a suitable number of such workers to each of the 'general casework' units may suffice. In deciding such a matter, much would depend upon one's judgment of the need for the unit supervisor herself to share such specialist expertise. It should be emphasised, however, that membership of a specialist unit would not imply that the workers concerned themselves exclusively with their own specialisms – the needs

FIGURE 3

A SUGGESTED ORGANISATIONAL STRUCTURE OF
A LOCAL AUTHORITY SOCIAL SERVICES AREA TEAM

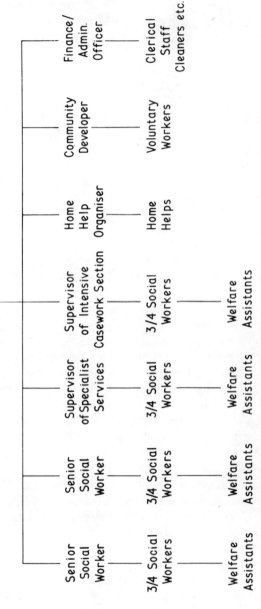

Area Social Worker

Senior Social Worker	Senior Social Worker	Supervisor of Specialist Services	Supervisor of Intensive Casework Section	Home Help Organiser	Community Developer	Finance/ Admin. Officer
3/4 Social Workers	3/4 Social Workers	3/4 Social Workers	3/4 Social Workers	Home Helps	Voluntary Workers	Clerical Staff Cleaners etc.
Welfare Assistants	Welfare Assistants	Welfare Assistants	Welfare Assistants			

NB: Specialist consultant functions can additionally be allotted where appropriate.

of the clients and families requiring a worker's especial skill are likely to extend beyond the need to learn Braille, for example, or acquire the facility to utilise special equipment. The specialist skill the worker possesses would be an *additional* skill. As the Seebohm Committee Report points out in paragraph 330 of its Report, '. . . the emphasis must be on helping the handicapped individual in the context of his family and community, and for this purpose a broadly based training approach will be required'.

The 'intensive casework unit', similarly, *could* be dispensed with if it were thought appropriate to do so, though such a step would need to be accompanied by a system of 'weighting' different kinds of case when deciding caseload size, which might be administratively difficult. The setting up of such a separate unit has been recommended in order to meet the needs of those families who require 'intensive casework' and rather more frequent visiting. A caseworker working exclusively with such families is unlikely to be able to carry a caseload much in excess of fifteen. Such workers could, from time to time, be interchanged with workers in the general casework units, if this were considered desirable, so that all workers could have the opportunity, if they wished, to gain some experience of this kind of work. Such a policy could mitigate any adverse effects specialisation might have upon promotion prospects and also contribute considerably to the opportunities for all staff to broaden their experience. It is likely that workers carrying a number of 'intensive' cases will need specialist support and leadership, and this may be an additional reason for setting up a specialist unit (with its own unit supervisor) to undertake intensive (and preventive) work with families, rather than to allocate a proportion of such cases to all the members of the 'general casework units', though it needs to be emphasised too that the Senior Social Workers heading 'general' units will also need to possess supervisory skills of a very high order.

The units within the Area Team which have so far been described are all likely to need to draw upon certain ancillary services. Among these are the Home Helps. The Seebohm Committee (in paragraph 590 of its Report) recommended that '. . . each area team would also have to include one or more home help organisers . . .' who would be responsible for a requisite number of home helps, and most Area Social

Workers are likely to place great importance upon this sector of their organisation, for it is now well recognised that the appropriate deployment of home help services can not only mitigate or prevent much human suffering and distress, but also in many cases avoid the necessity to split up families, or receive children or old people into care, It is possible that local authority social services departments, in formulating their policies, may decide that the home help service is one which needs expanding and that to invest greater resources in this sector may well result not only in a considerable reduction in human distress, but also a not inconsiderable reduction in local authority expenditure.

The appointment of trained home help supervisors to positions in the Area Team carrying equal status with the Senior Social Workers underlines the fact that such workers are seen as an integral part of the fieldwork and domiciliary services and as carrying out a very important social work function. The training and area of expertise of Home Help Supervisors are usefully described and discussed by Audrey Hunt (38).

Another unit within the Area Team structure is that concerned with community development. The Aves Committee Report (247) has stressed the opportunities which exist in the use of voluntary workers and it is appropriate that at area level there should be one officer taking responsibility for the allocation of volunteers to particular cases requiring their services. In this sense the Community Developer heads a unit which 'services' other units within the team, but his responsibilities extend far beyond this particular function. Although a member of the Area Team and, therefore, in the Sector controlled at Headquarters by the Assistant Director for Fieldwork and Domiciliary Services, the Community Developer at area level will need, for certain purposes, to work to the Assistant Director for Community and Staff Development. (This line of communication is not noted in Figures 2 and 3, but it will be important to ensure that any ambiguities arising from such dual control are clarified and resolved). The Seebohm Committee (in Chapter XVI of its Report) though emphasising the importance of providing a 'community-orientated service' with close links between itself and the community at all levels, did not spell out in organisational terms how this responsibility should be met. It did, however, select for special mention (in paragraph 503) the suggestion made to it by the Joint University Council for Social and Public Administration that '. . . at headquarters, under the director of a unified social service department, there should be an assistant director responsible for social development and public relations and *in close touch with area community development organisers working at the field level'* (authors' italics). The Committee observed that 'it would be well worth experimenting with such an organisational pattern, though many others may be considered'.

It is true, of course, that social workers especially skilled in 'community development' methods are in short supply. Training in this sphere of social work needs to be greatly expanded but in the meantime, as in the early days of case-work, experience may have to be gained without waiting upon formal training. This is a sector of social work activity in which there remain many unsolved problems (not the least of which consist in determining how to reconcile loyalty to one's local authority employers with assisting groups in the community in their conflicts *with* the local authority).

Another function of the Community Developer at area level might well be the collection of data concerning his area, ensuring that it is up to date and reliable, and feeding it up through the Area Social Worker to Headquarters, in prescribed form, so that an accurate 'portrait' may be drawn of the entire district for which the Department has responsibility. Social, demographic and epidemiological data, as well as data concerning resources and potential resources in the community which might be tapped, will be essential to policy making and to forward planning, and further reference is made to this in Chapter 6.

The delegation of maximum responsibility to the Area Social Workers almost certainly involves the delegation of certain powers over financial resources. The extent to which the power to spend money without reference to Headquarters must obviously vary from Department to Department and it is not possible here to make any firm recommendation. In addition to financial *powers* there will also be the question of financial *duties.* For example, in some departments it may be considered to be in the interests of efficiency, as well as desirable for other reasons, that the payment of foster mothers should be undertaken at area level rather than centralised at Headquarters.

In addition to financial matters, there will be a large number of other matters concerning the activities of the area team as a whole (statistics, records, clerical services and so on) for which it may be appropriate that a separate unit within the team should take responsibility, and as Figure 3 makes clear, it is envisaged that an Administrative Officer would head such a unit.

As with the Headquarters pattern, it is envisaged that the Area Social Worker and his unit leaders should form the Management Team for the Area, meeting regularly and concerning themselves with the overall activities of the Area workers so that these are fully co-ordinated. Such meetings of the Area Management Team would not, of course, remove the necessity for frequent unit meetings and team meetings taking place. The work of the Area Team needs to be *efficient,* in that it provides services to its clients and the community in an economic way; not by diminishing the quality or the range of service but by developing logical programmes and procedures and by trimming superflous activity. It should be *effective* in that it successfully attains the goals which have been determined for it. Each team member will need to understand this distinction and by regular meetings with colleagues and by other means, share both in the acceptance of the goals and of the means which are being, or need to be, employed to achieve them.

The setting up of the Area structure that has been described must necessarily involve a number of highly practical difficulties (quite apart from the psychological problems discussed in the previous chapter). The problem will be to effect a transition from one type of organisation to another while maintaining essential services and causing a minimum of distress or inconvenience to clients and families. Such an operation will need to be well planned and competently executed with as little delay as possible. A possible time-scale is presented in the next chapter.

While the majority of fieldworkers will be required, over a period of time, to give up functioning exclusively in their own prior specialism and to take on a more 'mixed' caseload, it will need to be recognised that the degree to which different workers will be able to achieve this in the short run may vary quite considerably, and it will be necessary, when allocating

Fig. 4. Temporary classification of basic grade social fieldworkers

Name	Area of previous experience	Professional qualif. or type of training	Length of experience	1st, 2nd and 3rd geographical preference	A Readiness & capacity to extend area of work. (Specify)	B Inability or marked reluctance to extend area of work	Remarks including potential and suitability for consultant role
	(e.g. Child Care; Mental Health; Welfare; Specialist work with blind or deaf, etc.)						

staff to particular area teams, and to particular units within them, to take account of their varying abilities and attitudes in this regard.

It is suggested, therefore, that irrespective of formal titles and salary grades, all workers be given a temporary classification which would indicate the area of their greatest competence, the areas in which they could function with some competence and their willingness and ability to take on additional areas of functioning. Such a scheme would be intended for use only in the *early* stages of the organisation of the Department; in time not only fieldworkers but 'cases' themselves would need to be free from 'labels' of this kind. A tentative grading scheme is set out in Figure 4.

4. Unifying Departmental Procedures

THE scale of operations to be undertaken by the Social Services Department of a Local Authority is likely to be considerable and social work administrators will need to get used to the idea that they are, in a sense, in 'big business'. Merging the resources of the existing social work agencies of a medium-sized local authority (with a population of, say, 250,000) may produce an annual revenue budget in the order of £1½ to £2 millions and a capital commitment of some £3 millions over the first five years. The manpower of such a combined Department may amount to as many as 2,000 staff if manual workers and part-time staff are included. Administrators responsible for large-scale organisations of this kind will need, therefore, to study the techniques which big business firms have found it necessary to adopt and be prepared to be influenced by principles of management theory. Many of these techniques and principles, however, have been promulgated within a context of profit-making enterprises and it will not be easy, initially for Directors and senior staff to find their way about these unfamiliar territories or to discover what may most usefully be borrowed or adapted. They may, however, be considerably helped by the fact that at this time something of a managerial revolution is taking place within local authorities as a whole and some expertise and experience is likely already to exist within the Chief Officers' Team.

The new department is likely to require that efficient accounting and budgeting systems should be incorporated and that programme planning should be undertaken in a logical and systematic way, perhaps applying network analysis techniques where appropriate. Punch-card systems for storing and handling statistics may prove useful in many departments, though in others it may be preferred to rely on the local authority computer. Algorithm charts may have an important part to play in assisting staff initially to learn unfamiliar procedures. Personnel management techniques may prove to be helpful in analysing jobs and in recruiting, training and evaluating staff.

This chapter, however, is concerned not so much with the application of new techniques as with the initial problems involved in bringing together into a 'unified' department different sets of independent, dissimilar procedures *which already exist* and, while maintaining 'business as usual', modifying and unifying them with the minimum of disruption to the ongoing work of the department. It is likely that, having grown up separately, the Children's Department and the Welfare Department (not to mention those parts of the Health and Mental Health Departments now to separate from a medical administration) will have developed very different sets of procedures even where similar activities are concerned. Their intake procedures will be different, their filing systems will be different, their methods of case-recording will be different, their forms, their 'returns', their statistics will be different. In many agencies it may be the case that the set procedures which are followed have not been written down but learned, as it were, 'by doing'. It is possible, even, that some procedures continue to be followed even though the necessity for them has long since disappeared. Certainly it will be the case that there will be no one individual in the new department who will be able to claim an overall acquaintance with or understanding of the entire range of procedures which will have been 'inherited'.

The Department will, in such circumstances, doubtless have to consider the long-term problem and the short-term problem separately. In the long term, the need to rationalise all departmental procedures will, of course, provide an unrivalled opportunity to examine them thoroughly and to develop a new set of procedures which will be modern, efficient, readily understood and consonant with the overall objectives of the department. In the short term the Department will be concerned to change only those procedures it is essential should be changed immediately, in order that the Department may function, and in changing them to ensure that all concerned in operating them are provided with opportunities to learn and understand them (which includes an understanding of the 'reason' for them).

Solving problems of this kind will constitute only a part of the many tasks facing the Director of the new Department, and in surveying the multiplicity and complexity of the tasks initially confronting him, he may well be forgiven for feeling initially overwhelmed or uncertain where to begin. Though by no means a *modern* management technique, the *compilation of a list of tasks* to be performed and the ordering of them into a logical sequence has much to commend it both psychologically and instrumentally. Psychologically because it can have the effect of shrinking the overall problem to some extent (even perhaps to manageable proportions) and induce a feeling of gaining some *control;* instrumentally because, put into a logical sequence, the list of tasks becomes the basis of a *programme.*

Divided into three phases ('Immediate', 'Intermediate' and 'Long-term') an example of such a list would be the following (though it is not intended to be more than an example and is not, therefore, by any means an exhaustive list):

Immediate (Planning Phase) – Duration approximately four months:
1. Personnel in the constituent departments carry on with their current work.
2. Appointment of Deputy and Assistant Directors.
3. Allocation of duties to Assistant Directors.
4. Appointment of Area Social Workers.
5. Two or three senior officers are relieved of their current duties and temporarily assigned to special planning duties under the Director.
6. An examination of current policies, programmes and procedures in the 'constituent departments' is begun by a 'working party', and short-term recommendations made.
7. An immediate review of all physical resources (buildings, equipment, etc.) which will accrue to the new department is undertaken by the Management Team, so that their best possible use in the future can be assessed.
8. Fieldworkers are classified according to their willingness and competence to take on a wide range of social

work functions (see Figure 4 on Page 51). (A note might also be made at the same time of possible training needs.) These temporary and confidential classifications would be independent of any salary grades and would be discarded in the long-term.

9. A similar initial review of existing day centre and residential staff is begun.
10. An initial examination of current active cases to determine if any clients or families are being seen by more than one worker is undertaken.
11. Immediate staffing needs are assessed.
12. A beginning is made on surveying community needs, problems, resources and potential.
13. Discussions with community leaders and other agencies are begun.
14. A tentative 'plan' is submitted to the Committee.
15. Decisions are made on the location of area teams.
16. The allocation of staff to area teams is decided.
17. All staff are given information concerning the situation as it exists and the tentative plans that have been drawn up for the immediate future.

Intermediate – Duration approximately eight months:
1. Community survey continues.
2. Discussions with community leaders and other agencies continue.
3. The allocation of cases to area teams is made.
4. Working party continues examination of 'procedures'.
5. Recruitment programme for 'volunteers' is drawn up.
6. A detailed review of institutions, day centres, etc., the services offered, present staffing, procedures in force, etc., is undertaken.
7. Examination of current cases within areas is undertaken and recategorisation, where appropriate, decided.
8. Further unification of forms and procedures decided.
9. Lines of communication are formalised.
10. Training needs are comprehensively examined.
11. An initial departmental manual is produced.
12. Staffing needs are re-assessed.
13. Short-term in-service training courses are initiated.
14. Initial research projects are planned and begun.

Long-term
1. A 'social portrait' of the district is completed.
2. Long-term social needs are assessed.
3. A review and evaluation of earlier plans, policies, and programmes is undertaken.
4. Further unification of procedures takes place within the Department.
5. Research for next five years is planned.
6. Long-term recruitment and training policy is developed.
7. The future role of local voluntary organisations vis-a-vis the Department is examined.
8. Development plans for the next quinquennium are drawn up, with tentative estimates of cost.

In these examples of 'tasks to be performed' they have not necessarily been placed in a strict order of priority, and of course many of them may need to be undertaken simultaneously. In view of the number of activities in the Immediate and Intermediate phases and the necessity for their harmonious development and appropriate timing, it may be useful to programme major tasks on a time-scale chart, as in Figure 5. A moveable cursor can then indicate the extent to which performance of tasks is up to or behind schedule.

It is not possible here to discuss these 'tasks' in any detail and indeed many of them are self-explanatory. Some, however, though the need to undertake them may be obvious, will present, in practice, considerable difficulties. How, for example, should the department set about the task of discovering which of its innumerable cases are currently the concern of several workers? How (and when) should it set about discovering from its closed cases in one constituent department information which would be helpful in dealing with a current case in another? How should it set about 'unifying' its filing system and allocating cases appropriately to the newly constituted area teams? What criteria should it employ in deciding how much information should be filed at Headquarters and how much in the residential home or area office? Should it in the short run tolerate a situation which allows staff to claim expenses or submit mileage returns on a multiplicity of different forms? Should it decide that, from the outset, at least all new cases should have a uniform 'intake face-sheet' and uniform card-index cards?

57

FIGURE 5

EXAMPLES OF 'TASKS TO BE PERFORMED'

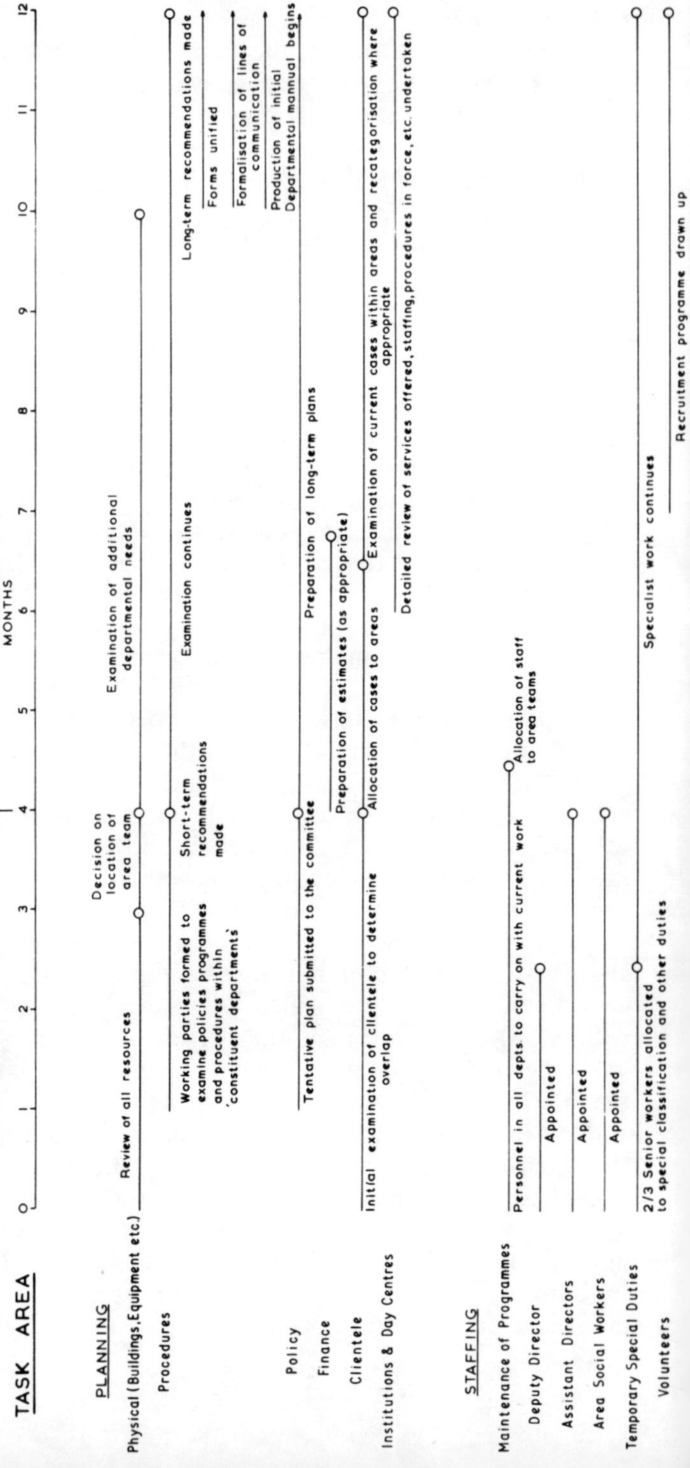

STAFF EVALUATION & TRAINING

Fieldworkers   Classified   Allocated   Supervision schemes instituted

Residential Workers   Classified   Allocated   Supervision schemes instituted

Assessment of Need   Immediate needs   Needs re-assessed

Training   In service—training begins

RESEARCH

Community Survey   Preliminary report

Projects   Continues / Projects begin

COMMUNICATIONS

With Staff — Regular discussions, visits to offices and institutions, institution of regular "news sheet"

With Committee & Other Local Authority Departments — Reports as appropriate or when requested. Regular contact, inter-departmental meetings, conferences etc.

With Government — Reports as legally required or as requested

With Other Agencies & Community Leaders — Frequent contact and discussion both formally and informally

CODE

The commencement of a line [————] indicates the start of a process.
The circle O indicates the time at which it is planned that some process or task should be completed. It can be filled in [●] when done.
If used as a wall chart a moveable cursor can indicate which tasks are behind schedule — ie. those to the left of the cursor still marked [O]

Many of these practical problems will be capable of solution only after full discussion between knowledgeable members of staff from the various constituent departments. Certainly it is not possible in this Chapter to provide global answers, But it is important that the questions should be posed. Let us take the first question as an example. How should the department set about the task of discovering in which of the current cases it has 'inherited' there is overlapping? To compile lists of cases, even if restricted to basic information concerning name, address and reference number, would be an extremely time-consuming operation, and even when compiled there would still be considerable practical problems involved in deciding how best to compare the lists. To use existing card indexes might have the merit of facilitating sorting and comparison, but would have the disadvantage of completely disrupting the existing systems before they could be replaced with a new one. Moreover, it may be the case that *addresses* will be as important as names (families can contain members bearing different names; it might be helpful to know about links which exist between different families; it would be useful to learn that a particular foster parent was also a client of another constituent department; and so on). How then might addresses be compared? At first sight this looks like a job for the computer, though the task of preparing the computer programme and feeding in the data would be an extremely formidable one. A possible solution (owing nothing to modern management techniques but having the great merit of comparative simplicity) would be for each of the constituent departments to note the reference number of any existing case (and in different coloured ink the reference number of any closed case) against the name and address of the family concerned in the electoral register for the district. The electoral registers could then be compared and any overlapping noted immediately. This system would also have the merit of providing information by *electoral wards* and indicate the distribution of cases. Doubtless there would be some cases for which there was not an electoral register entry, though even with these the *address* would be likely to figure in the register, and a separate note could be made of these cases. Care would have to be taken, of course, when noting closed cases, for doubtless some of these families will have moved, but even this would come to light fairly easily, since in carrying out the comparison of lists one would be working primarily from the live cases.

Once a list had been compiled of the cases where over-lapping existed, the files themselves could be brought together and decisions taken concerning their future allocation and the manner in which the 'transfer' of worker should be facilitated. The allocation of existing cases to area teams will itself be an exercise requiring considerable forethought and planning, even where no overlapping exists, since the allocation of staff and the allocation of cases to a particular area team will not always coincide. In some authorities one constituent depart-ment may have been divided into three areas while another constituent department has been divided into four, so that some transfers of cases from one worker to another will be inevitable in addition to the transfers from several workers to only one.

While on the subject of the review of cases, it may be apposite to mention that the review of closed cases may have value other than to discover whether any of them are live cases in another sector of the organisation. The Seebohm Committee Report has reminded us that it will be a respon-sibility of the new unified department not only to meet need, but also to detect it, and this has been a theme of several other Government Reports. Closed cases which come under review may often enable us to deduce possible new needs which may be worth investigating or provide us with infor-mation which we can add to other accumulated data and discover, perhaps, that a fresh approach to the individual or family concerned is indicated.

The departmental filing system is one of the most important and powerful instruments it has at its disposal for assisting decision taking, for detecting needs, for appropriately meeting needs, for allocating its resources optimally, and for learning from its mistakes. Yet social work departments, though tradi-tionally wedded to the vast accumulation of data concerning their clients and the recording of lengthy accounts of each and every encounter with them, have not up to now been especially adept in using their records intelligently. Indeed, filing cabinets are everywhere crammed with files so bulky that few are ever read and the recording of information is undertaken by some staff for reasons of bureaucratic con-formity rather than in any expectation that it will be of value to themselves, their clients or the organisation as a whole.

The problem confronting the administrators in the new departments however will not initially be to discover the optimum use to which existing records may be put, but simply to decide how best to bring several different filing systems and systems of data-recording together into one uniform system and to accomplish this task in such a way that the ongoing work of the department is not unduly disrupted and quick access to essential information impeded.

In the short run, it will probably be wise to maintain existing card indexes intact, though taking care to amend reference numbers where these are changed on the files themselves, so that files may be quickly traced. It may be desirable from the outset to introduce a uniform 'face-sheet' for every new case and gradually to make out similar 'face-sheets' for all existing live cases, giving priority to cases in which more than one 'constituent department' has been concerned. In these latter types of case the various files will need to be 'brought together', a summary prepared and a new 'file identity' and reference number allocated.

So far as possible, existing case-record 'forms' should continue to be used, though 'headed-up' by the new face sheet containing essential basic data. In the long term it may be necessary to abolish or replace some case-record 'forms' as well as a number of general departmental forms, and introduce re-designed ones more appropriate to the 'generic' nature of the department's activities. Recommendations to do this will doubtless arise in a number of ways and from a number of sources, as experience is gained, but it may be useful to channel all ideas and suggestions concerning this subject through a specially constituted 'working party', Except where absolutely essential, a reasonable time should elapse, during which experience may be gained and evaluated, before introducing changes of this kind.

So far as card index systems are concerned, it may be useful to distinguish between cards whose purpose is to act as a 'signpost' to the exact location of information stored elsewhere (e.g. in a file) and cards whose purpose is to carry information and facilitate 'counting'. In the second category come 'punched cards', for example, and whether used for storing information destined to be fed into a computer, or for more modest purposes (hand or mechanical sorting and counting within the department itself), these can make a big contribution to sound administration.

A small card measuring approximately 7¼ x 3¼ inches can carry a very large number of items of information since they are normally divided into 10 rows each of 80 columns. They can thus be particularly useful in enabling one to isolate particular variables in a large number of cases and to discover associations between variables. They are also helpful when undertaking tasks which need to be carried out regularly – compiling statistics, under a number of different heads, of children in care, for example.

Systems of this kind, however, depend for their efficiency upon the accuracy of the data fed into them. Experience would indicate that where errors occur they are less likely to be attributable to faulty 'punching' or faulty 'counting', than to errors in the written 'returns' provided by field or residential staff from which the data are extracted. Errors of this kind are themselves often the result, not so much of carelessness as such, as of an 'attitude of mind' about statistics or about being required to render 'returns'. Collecting statistics, for many social workers, is an unwelcome 'chore', and they feel like this about it because, in so many cases, the information they collect for a 'remote administration' is never seen or heard of again (except when there is an error, and then they are called to account). It cannot be sufficiently stressed how dependent accuracy is upon attitude, and how, in turn, attitude depends upon 'feed-back'. It is the responsibility of all administrators who require statistical information to be fed to them that they ensure that (a) the staff from whom the information is sought know *why* it is being sought, and (b) in due time, staff are provided with some 'feed-back' (i.e. the lessons learned from a consideration of the data are shared with the personnel providing the information).

Reference was made in Chapter 2 to the difficulties some staff are likely to experience in adapting to new procedures which may be introduced for the carrying out of familiar tasks and the difficulties they may experience in learning the procedures to be followed when performing new tasks. Workers may be helped in overcoming these kinds of difficulty if 'set procedures' are laid down in written form for ready reference by those needing to familiarise themselves with them. Sometimes a 'set procedure' will simply consist of a

FIGURE 6

EXAMPLE OF A PROCEDURE
SET OUT IN AN ALGORITHM FORM
MENTAL HEALTH ACT 1959

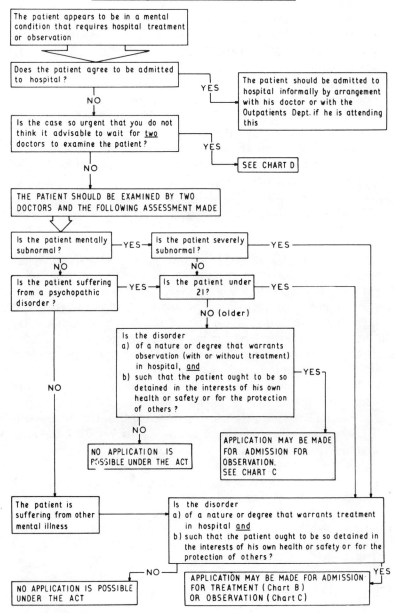

check-list of 'things to be done', for example:

Admission to residential care (elderly person)
1. Personal Record Folder completed.
2. Personal Record Folder serial number allocated.
3. Index card prepared for central registry.
4. Guidance leaflet given to resident.
5. Pensions and Allowances verified.
6. Capital resources allocated.
7. Pension/allowance books submitted for re-grading.
8. Agency authorisation necessary?
9. Personal allowances arranged.
10. Method of payment determined.
11. Financial control sheet prepared.
12. Accomodation register entry.
13. Medical record card checked.
14. Medical classification established.
15. Maintenance Register entered.
16. G.P. advised of admission.
17. Personal property protected.

It will be noted that in such a check-list only administrative activities are included. Plainly the admission to residential care of an elderly person will involve one or more of the department's workers undertaking other essential work with the client (and with his family). These (casework) activities, which are likely to be concerned with preparing the elderly person to come to terms with his need to leave home and enter a residential establishment, with settling him in, with coping with family feelings in the matter, and so on, are not matters which can be listed in a set of procedures, they will be activities pertinent to a particular case, and will be appropriately recorded in the casework file in the Area Office, or in the file kept at the residential establishment.

Not all 'procedures', of course, can be reduced to a simple list, as in the above example. Sometimes a worker will be faced with a series of 'administrative choices' or 'decisions' (if A, then B, C, or D can follow, if B is decided upon then E and F flow therefrom, whereas if C, then G or H has to be implemented, and so on). In complicated sets of 'procedures' of this kind, it may be helpful to workers needing to familiarise themselves with them, to set each out in the form of an 'algorithm'. Figure 6 is a relatively simple example, and related to a procedure to be adopted for admission to hospital under the Mental Health Act, 1959. As it is an example only, the Charts B, C and D referred to in the Figure have not been included.

More complicated sets of procedures can, of course, also be set out in this way and another use to which the technique can be put is in the designing of 'forms'.

Another set of procedures which will need to be introduced are those relating to *evaluation*. The word, of course, can mean many things and although it will sometimes be desirable to assess the value in financial terms of this or that service, or to compare the relative financial costs of achieving a given end by alternative means, this is by no means all that is involved in the concept of 'evaluation'. While it is true that social service agencies are not motivated by considerations of profit-making, as commercial enterprises predominantly are, not all aspects of commercial organisations lend themselves to evaluation in financial terms either. The public relations department, the personnel department, the long range planning department in a commercial undertaking, though doubtless contributing to the firm's efficiency and therefore to its profitability, are not themselves normally seen exclusively in profit-making terms, and if their activities are to be evaluated, criteria other than of a financial kind have to be applied.

So it is with a social services department. Social service organisations need, then, to devise procedures which are capable of evaluating the effectiveness of (a) the department as a totality; (b) different sectors of the total organisation; and (c) individual members of staff. And broadly they can do this only by measuring the degree to which explicitly stated specific goals are in fact achieved within the time which has been allowed for their achievement, and within their budget allocation.

So far as the department as a totality is concerned, it will be necessary to devise procedures for (a) spelling out in broad terms the objectives of the Department as a whole; (b) translating these into a series of 'specifics'; (c) ascertaining and recording what has, in fact, been achieved in pursuing them; and (d) comparing (b) and (c) by applying criteria which are both quantitative and qualitative in character.

A similar set of procedures will also need to be devised for assessing the effectiveness of each 'sector' of the organisation;

although here, of course, we shall be concerned less with broad departmental objectives and more with detailed specific sector activities (e.g. the extent to which the intention to develop and implement an improved system of making payments to foster mothers has been realised).

At the individual level staff evaluation may also be a matter of some importance. It is not proposed to discuss this subject here, beyond making the point that before introducing such a procedure (as with the others) it will be important to be very clear about one's reasons for doing so, and about the purposes to which the knowledge gained are to be put. It will also be important to discuss this procedure and the reasons for it with the staff themselves.

While on the subject of evaluation, it may be useful to consider another aspect. One of the dangers, perhaps, of evaluating a service is that one may pay too much attention to the 'providers' of that service. (How well are they doing the job they have been given to do? In what ways could they be helped to do it better?, and so on.) But it may be that the job they have been given to do is the *wrong* job, or is being performed by the wrong people, or that the service is being given *to* the wrong people. It may be important, then, to consider not only the effectiveness of a service *given,* but also the quantity and quality of a service *received;* to view the matter, that is to say, not from the 'provider' end, but from the 'consumer' end. For example, instead of (or perhaps as well as) evaluating the effectiveness of the work of the 'home help sector' of the organisation, we should consider specific groups of 'consumers' in the community and seek to ascertain whether we are (a) discovering them; (b) identifying their needs; and (c) meeting their needs in the best possible ways, giving them what they need in sufficient quantity, of sufficiently high quality, and at the right time.

Figure 7 takes the elderly as an example and presents in schematic outline the relationships which exist between the several procedures which may be involved in assessing the service provided for and received by this particular group of clients and potential clients. As can be seen, it is a complicated network, and is concerned not only with the extent to which known needs are being met (and how well) but also with the extent to which unexpressed needs might best be discovered. It will also be noted that the outline provides for different

67

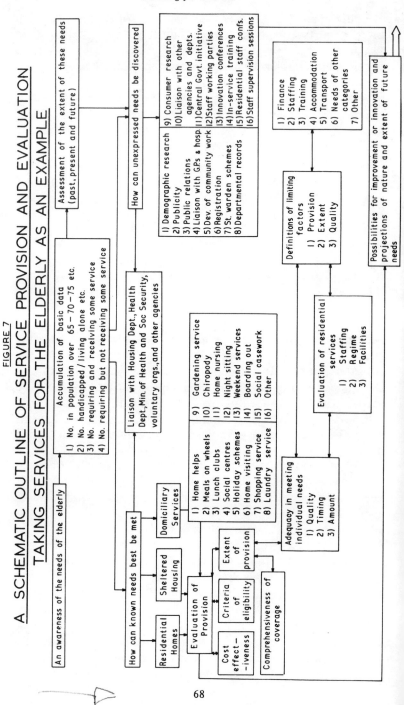

FIGURE 7

A SCHEMATIC OUTLINE OF SERVICE PROVISION AND EVALUATION TAKING SERVICES FOR THE ELDERLY AS AN EXAMPLE

kinds of evaluation at different *levels* (e.g. cost effectiveness; the overall comprehensiveness of a particular service; its adequacy in meeting individual need; its timing; the facilities provided, the staffing, and the 'regime' of particular residential establishments; and so on). This is another way of saying that it is not sufficient to evaluate the overall comprehensiveness of a service. Many other tests also have to be applied. For example, the meals-on-wheels service may be reaching 100% of the old people needing it, but if it is providing only two meals a week to large numbers of clients who need seven, or if the meals themselves are of poor quality, or arrive at the wrong time of day, then we may wish to consider ways in which the service might be improved, or it may be, partly supplemented, perhaps by the provision of more or better lunch-club facilities.

In this Chapter a number of general and specific ideas have been presented on the subject of departmental procedures. As with the book as a whole, no attempt has been made to provide a comprehensive 'blueprint' and there will be large numbers of different procedures to be considered by individual Directors and their staffs for which no space has been found for discussion here. This is, of course, inevitable, though it is hoped that what has been said may provide some indication of a possible approach to these problems.

5. In-service Training
and In-service Learning

AN IMPORTANT factor in the development of Social Services
Departments will be the extent to which their staffs are comprised of professionally trained personnel, but inasmuch as
Departments will be in competition in attracting such staff
and the number of professionally trained workers is likely,
for as long as can be foreseen, to fall far short of the demand,
most departments will have to operate with a staff partly
made up of trained and partly of untrained workers. Some of
these trained workers may lack experience, some of the untrained may be highly experienced, and as both training and
experience are likely to have been acquired for the most
part in single specialist settings of all kinds, it can readily be
seen that the training needs of field staff within a new department are likely to be extremely diverse. Some untrained staff
may subsequently be seconded for professional training on
the various types of training course which it is envisaged the
new Council for Education and Training in Social Work will
be encouraging, but aside from the provision of *professional*
training (either for fieldwork or for residential work) it is
likely that there will be considerable need for *in-service*
training courses of all kinds to be provided for all staff,
whether or not they have been professionally trained, whether
or not they are awaiting professional training, whether or not
they are workers of long experience for whom professional
training will not now be appropriate.

Broadly speaking, therefore, Social Services Departments
are likely to be involved in two main kinds of training
activity:

    (a)   the provision of fieldwork or residential training
          placements for students on professional courses; and

(b) a wide variety of in-service training courses for different categories of staff, mounted and staffed by the department itself, or in collaboration with other nearby departments (and possibly calling upon some assistance from local university or technical college resources).

Since this chapter is concerned with *in-service* training, it is not proposed to discuss (a) beyond noting that in Figure 2 on page 34 it is envisaged that both (a) and (b) could conveniently be made the responsibility of the same Assistant Director.

Chapter 2 of this book outlined the many different types of change to which all the staff in the new department will need to adjust, and pointed to the need for the provision by the department of help to staff in achieving such adjustments through the medium of in-service training courses and in other ways. Inasmuch as successful integration entails a sharing of specialist knowledge and skills and the adoption of a 'generic' approach by all concerned, it is likely that, using the term 'in-service training' in its widest sense, *all* personnel will benefit from participation in it.

Some personnel, entering the new department without training or previous experience, will need the provision of a broadly-based induction course extending perhaps over six to nine months on a one-day-a-week basis, preceded and followed perhaps by two two-week blocks of concentrated study. The outline syllabus of such a course designed for workers in the Health and Welfare Services (145) provides an example of what is here envisaged, though in view of the wider responsibilities to be undertaken in the new department, it would be necessary to revise and extend it appropriately, giving greater weighting to the child care content but also emphasising very much more a 'generic', family-oriented approach to local authority social work.

Other personnel, either trained or experienced in a particular specialism and thus already possessing some basic social work knowledge, will need a variety of opportunities for broadening their orientation and acquiring knowledge and skills in different 'specialisms'. Such needs may be catered for to some extent (as will be described later) in individual supervision. in informal contacts between staff, in case conference discussions, in area team meetings, and perhaps in membership of working parties set up to deal with specific problems, but in addition to these media, it is likely that the provision of more formal training courses – perhaps on a half-day a week basis – will be necessary.

In-service training provision of this kind might be achieved by providing courses in specific disciplines designed to fill gaps in specialist knowledge ('Child Care for Welfare Officers', etc.) but this approach is not recommended. Although it is possible that some lectures concerned with legislation and specific aspects of social policy might be needed by some categories of staff and not others (i.e. trained ex-child care staff might not need to attend lectures on child care legislation) it is probable that a better approach might be to provide courses for *mixed groups.* Such courses could draw upon particular expertise possessed by group members but would seek to emphasise common features of social work practice rather than differences. Taught well, such courses could assist enormously, not only in making essential *knowledge* available, but also in widening the horizons of all concerned, enabling them to move away from the symptom-centred approach which their former agency-function may have imposed upon them.

It is not proposed here to go into any detail concerning the *content* of such courses, since this will be partly dictated by the particular needs of staff members. In Chapter 4 it was recommended that the opportunity should be taken to make a note of training needs, when reviewing staff resources in order to decide upon optimum deployment, and plainly it will be one of the first tasks of the Assistant Director responsible for training to undertake a review both of training needs and of training resources (both within and without the Department) to meet those needs.

In assessing the training needs of staff it will be important to consider *all* staff. Senior members of staff will need to be catered for no less than junior staff, though it may well be that their needs will be different. In some departments it may be appropriate to divide up staff, for this purpose, as follows:

1. Senior Staff
2. Student supervisors
3. Potential student supervisors
4. Field staff
5. Day Centre staff ⎱ (These might need to be further sub-
6. Residential staff ⎰ divided)

7. Receptionists and other ancillary staff
8. Home Helps
9. Volunteers

Some of these categories might be better catered for within the department, others by attendance at courses in local university extra-mural departments or technical college social work departments. They are listed here only to emphasise that *all* categories of staff are likely to have some training needs and none should be overlooked. It is possible, of course, that some staff members might find themselves included in more than one in-service training activity – for example, a professionally trained child care officer with two or three years' experience of working in a child care department might attend a course for 'potential student supervisors' provided in a nearby University department and also a 're-orientation course' within the Social Services Department itself.

It may be appropriate within the context of this Chapter to introduce the concept of 'in-service learning', because plainly 'learning' is of greater importance than 'training' inasmuch as it is the desired 'end-product'. It is also a much *wider* concept. In-service learning is a derivative of in-service training, but it can also be derived from many other activities. In a sense, of course, one can learn from all one's experiences, both within the agency and elsewhere, but in order to maximise learning and ensure that it is systematised and appropriately exploited, it may be necessary, consciously, deliberately and as a matter of departmental policy, to provide for all staff (*in addition* to in-service training opportunities) a variety of in-service learning opportunities as well.

How might this be done? The first thing that needs to be done is to create a climate of opinion favourable to the concept of learning – a departmental spirit, a social services ethos, of which a major characteristic will be the acceptance of and enthusiasm about the need to learn, and the placing of learning high in the value-system of the department as a whole.

In-service learning, as has been said, can be acquired in all kinds of ways, ways which will include attendance on in-service training courses, ways which will be independent of such courses, ways which will be incidental to them, and ways which will affect and be affected by them. One important way is through individual supervision; another is through participation in multi-disciplinary case-conferences in which experience in case presentation can be gained and a great deal learned from the variety of opinion expressed by colleagues. It needs to be emphasised, however, that successful learning from either individual supervision or group case-discussion may be highly dependent upon the qualities and skills possessed by the supervisor or group-leader (and this, in turn, may have implications for departmental policy in regard to the need to equip suitable personnel in the department to undertake these tasks by giving *them* appropriate in-service training).

Both individual supervision and group discussions are capable of promoting and enhancing learning in a number of ways. A worker learns, of course, a certain amount from his experience of working with a client. In the process of recording his work with the client, it is likely that further learning takes place; in presenting his work for discussion with a supervisor, or with a colleague group, still further learning is promoted, and from the ensuing discussions, still more. In the individual supervision sessions, moreover, a worker is likely to enter into a professional relationship with his supervisor which, in some respects, is analogous to a casework relationship, and thereby is enabled to take from it not only an enhanced intellectual understanding of his work but also a deeper understanding of his own professional self. Although it needs to be emphasised that it is no part of the supervisor's function to 'casework' a supervisee, we may nevertheless point to the following similarities between the two activities:

1. Supervision is exercised through the use of an ongoing professional relationship.
2. The supervisory relationship is characterised by the supervisor's desire to help the worker to function more effectively, to solve problems, and/or to understand himself and his activities more clearly;
3. Supervision is carried out through the medium of interviews which:
   (a) are held regularly over a period of time, usually arranged by appointment to suit the convenience of both parties;
   (b) are on a one-to-one basis; and
   (c) involve the supervisor being visited by the worker, or vice-versa, or both;

4. Supervision is characterised by certain principles, e.g.:
   (a) the principle of confidentiality (though this is not absolute – nor is it in casework):
   (b) the principle of self-determination;
   (c) the principle of individualisation;
   (d) the principle of acceptance;
   and so on.
5. Effective supervision calls for certain casework understanding and casework skills;
6. Effective supervision may call for the deployment of certain procedures and techniques, analogous to those in casework, e.g.
   (a) sustaining procedures;
   (b) direct influence;
   (c) catharsis or ventilation;
   (d) reflective consideration of current realities;
   (e) helping the worker to look at himself;
7. The appropriate selection of supervisory procedures and techniques is governed by similar criteria as those used in casework.

Essential differences between the two activities will include the following:
1. The worker will not necessarily have sought the help of the supervisor;
2. The focus of the interview is on the worker's work, not on his personal history or personal affairs;
3. Although, as in casework, much of the transaction between supervisor and supervisee will be verbal (and non-verbal too in the interactional sense) there will, in supervision, also be considerable use of and interpretation of *recorded* material.

So far as *group discussion* is concerned, not only may the worker himself be enabled to learn from colleagues, and (if the group is made up of workers with disparate experience or a variety of trainings) to gain a much wider perspective than he may previously have possessed, but learning will also take place within the group as a whole. Indeed group activity of this kind, focussed on cases rather than on 'curricular subjects', can provide, if well led, an extremely enriching experience for every individual taking part. It cannot be said too often that what in the long run has to be learned by all concerned is not represented by the 'sum of the parts' but a view of social work and social work method which transcends that sum.

Another method of 'In-service learning' will be *consultation* and it will be important that everyone within the Department should recognise that seeking information or advice from others is an activity to be encouraged, not something to be frowned upon. Knowledge and expertise are likely to reside in different individuals and at all levels in the organisation and will need to be made freely available. It is essential, however, that consultation and supervision should not be confused. They are quite different activities, though the former term is often used (quite wrongly) as a euphemism for the latter. Among the more important differences between consultation and supervision are:

1. consultation is ad hoc and concerned with single isolated problems; supervision is ongoing and regular and concerned with the whole spectrum of a worker's work;
2. consultation implies that the initiative for calling the meeting between worker and consultant lies with the worker;
3. consultation implies that the decision about the discussion content between worker and consultant is taken by the worker;
4. consultation implies that the worker is aware that he has a problem, whereas supervision sometimes focusses upon hitherto unrecognised difficulties.

It can thus be seen that, although consultation facilities need to be made widely available to all staff, and their use encouraged, in no sense can consultation be an acceptable substitute for supervision.

When thinking about in-service learning, we should not overlook the many opportunities that are provided by quite informal meetings between staff-members and the many discussions that take place in the staff room over cups of coffee. As a method of 'learning', such contacts should by no means be despised – they are not just useful, they are essential. This provides, perhaps, an additional reason for deciding upon the formation of 'inter-disciplinary teams', but it may need to be remembered that some groups of workers (in residential establishments and day centres, for example) may be more isolated and need to be provided with opportunities for social (as well as formal and semi-formal) contacts with other kinds of worker.

In-service learning may also depend upon the receipt of information and ideas in written form and it is desirable, therefore, that attention should be given to the various methods that may exist for providing this. It is likely that the Departmental Headquarters will need to issue both a periodical *Bulletin* of information and *Circular Instructions* on specific subjects. The staff may themselves decide to publish a non-official staff journal. Access both to essential books and professional journals may need to be facilitated by the establishment of a departmental library. A Manual of Procedure or Departmental Handbook which will codify and bring together policy directives and instructions, information concerning the organisation of the department and its several responsibilities and basic data concerning the area itself, will prove of enormous value to all concerned, provided it is produced in such a way that necessary amendments to keep it up to date can fairly easily be made.

Thought needs to be given to the induction of new members of staff, not only in terms of an in-service training course of the kind referred to on page 71, but also to equip them with written material containing essential facts. New members of staff are customarily introduced to colleagues, but it is often difficult for them later to remember who was who. A list of staff members, their room and telephone numbers, and their roles and functions; a list of other agencies, with telephone numbers; a map of the district, a departmental handbook; a complete set of bulletins and circulars, all these can be of immense help to the newcomer in his endeavour to remember and make sense of the mass of verbal information which is so often thrown at him during his first few days in the department. Indeed material of this kind may be very helpful to all members of staff during the early months of the department's existence!

Another essential medium of communication and in-service learning is the staff meeting. Not only should regular meetings of area teams, of residential staffs, of day-centre staff, of HQ staff, of Area Social Workers, of Residential and Day Centre Heads, and so on, be encouraged (even required) to take place, but from time-to-time (perhaps annually) a full staff conference should be mounted. Participation in working parties to consider specific subjects has also been mentioned as an important activity, and this too can provide valuable opportunities for 'learning'. Small conferences on specific themes may possibly also have a part to play – *innovation conferences,* for example, at which the 'game' to be played is the creation of an entirely new method of meeting a particular need, or *evaluation conferences,* at which a particular aspect of service (say, services for old people) comes under critical scrutiny over an extended period of time.

In this chapter we have been concerned to emphasise that there are many ways of assisting staff to develop professionally; that providing in-service training, important though it is, is only one way and needs to be underpinned by a number of other devices; that professional development would be very lopsided if it meant only development in the acquisition of specific skills; and that as important as the learning of skills and the acquiring of knowledge is the development of certain attitudes. Senior staff in the new departments, to whom this small book is principally addressed, have a large responsibility in this matter, for senior staff are very influential. Like parents, the way they behave is noted – and imitated! In their informal contacts with subordinates, no less than in their formal ones, senior staff will be continually promoting (or hindering) the professional development of others – the way they behave in a staff meeting, the manner in which they speak of clients, the attitudes they reveal, the things they say over cups of tea, the books and journals they read, or make available to others, the example they set – in a thousand and one different situations – all these are subtly influential. One could go on adding to the list of ways in which, consciously or unconsciously, a senior member may turn a raw, green recruit (or an experienced but bewildered former specialist) into a competent worker in an integrated department – the encouragement he is given, the value placed upon 'learning', the extent to which his supervisors behave professionally, the extent to which he is helped to understand his place in the organisation and the place of others, the extent to which he is prevented from misunderstanding – the list is endless!

6. Agency-based Research

IN THE social work agencies of this country, hundreds of decisions are taken every day that, for good or ill, will affect the lives of people. These decisions are likely to be largely determined by the individual personality, training and experience of those taking them and they are unlikely to be much influenced by any systematic research.

Research plays an important role in many professions and in many aspects of our daily lives but, as yet, is relatively insignificant in the social work profession. There are three possible reasons why this should be so. The first is that the profession has investigated research, has weighed it in the balance, has found it to be wanting and has rejected it. The second is that the profession, having considered the matter, has decided that a systematic study of itself, what it is doing, and to whom and how well, is either unnecessary or too threatening. The third possibility is that no conscious thought has been given to the matter.

If one looks at some of the research findings that are available and asks how this or that particular finding actually helps one to do one's job better, how it can enable one to act differently with clients, then there may be some justification for rejecting research because, from a strictly utilitarian point of view, its contribution so far has probably been marginal. But to reject research on the basis of its contribution to date is really to miss the point. Research method is comprised of a logical sequence of disciplined activities which may be identified as the formulation of an existing problem, formulating hypotheses, defining concepts, establishing working definitions, designing the study, (including the development of a valid data-gathering design), collecting data, measuring results, interpreting findings, and reporting. Moving systematically, in this way, from step to step, enables the research worker to make knowledge available which did not exist before, knowledge which may enable informed decisions to be taken rather than leaps in the dark. Research as a method of knowing by systematically finding out cannot logically be rejected simply because it may not always have been used well in the past. One might equally reject the science of psychology simply because a salesman has used (or misused) it to sell an unwanted vacuum cleaner to a reluctant housewife.

Until recently research method has not been included as an essential subject in the curricula of social work training courses. This is now beginning to be seen as important, not only because it is desirable that research into social work should be undertaken by some social workers, but also because it is desirable that *all* social workers should be able to read, understand and evaluate social work research undertaken by others. At present it is the case that social workers, as a group, do not read and are not influenced by research findings. Unless this trend is reversed the future for social work cannot be bright.

It seems likely that research is not regarded as an important tool by social workers, not so much because they suspect it as a valid approach to collecting information or because there is a total ignorance about it, as that they fail to see the relevance of the information it provides. Viewing the client as a unique being, generalisations, or statements about collections of people, are not seen as helpful, though, paradoxically, trained social workers seem to have little difficulty in accepting general psycho-analytic theory as having widespread individual relevance.

Over the years, however, as social workers, we develop our own ways of working; our own ways of doing things. We form our own convictions, our own prejudices. We may think we know, for example, that couples who adopt a baby are more likely to have one of their own within a year or two, or that the man who is always threatening to kill himself is not likely to carry out his threat. The great problem with our convictions, however, is we can feel quite sure about their essential 'rightness' even when they are completely wrong. as, indeed, both these are! Convictions are hard to give up, even in the face of contrary evidence. So, if one has known a number of couples who have had their own child soon after adopting a baby, one is reluctant to accept research findings which indicate that one's experience was misleading. To shed a treasured belief that one has nurtured and cherished throughout one's professional life is like losing an arm. We do not give it up without a struggle. But usually there is no-one to struggle with us and we continue to hold our often quite groundless assumptions regardless of their inaccuracies. And even when more accurate information is available to us, we claim to be far too busy to read it.

We can do this because social work does not seem to depend for its continuance upon end-results. We say that the client and his well-being is the reason for our professional existence and that our agency is client-centred but in reality, not all of our subsequent activity is in harmony with this. In some of the better agencies, where supervision is taken seriously, it is possible that worker and supervisor may go carefully through one particular case to try to see where things went wrong and how the worker might perhaps have done better, but this, it would seem, is still the exception rather than the rule. Still fewer agencies systematically look at all their cases (or a random sample of them) and attempt to 'tease out' those factors that are statistically associated with failure, in an attempt to formulate more effective agency policies, procedures or techniques. A child comes into care, is placed in one foster home but does not settle; she is placed in another, has a short spell in an institution, is moved to another foster home, and so on, with no-one pulling out pertinent data and adding it to the data collected on the comings and goings of other children in order to see whether or not these data have a story to tell us or a lesson to teach.

One reason why social work within an agency is rarely systematically studied is the philosophy that each case must be regarded as unique. It is true, of course, that each case *is* unique, but this in no way entails that several cases do not have common features. Another reason (perhaps flowing from the first) is that agencies tend not to have overall objectives for which to strive. Workers are given tasks to perform but not goals to attain. We think about the giving of a service but not about managing an agency in order to attain its global objectives. In dealing with human beings it is not easy to develop methods of adequately and accurately measuring what is being done, and even where measurement is attempted, or statistics collected, little if anything is done to interpret their meaning (226) or to use the findings in order to modify agency policy. The explanation given is usually that we are too busy. Too busy doing what we are doing to attempt to understand what we are doing, why we are doing it, whether we are in fact doing what we think we are doing, and whether it is doing any good!

Some lip service is now being paid to the value of research in social work. The Seebohm Committee, for example, states (in paragraph 455):

'We have made it clear in several chapters how much importance we attach to research. The personal social services are large scale experiments in ways of helping those in need. It would be both wasteful and irresponsible to set experiments in motion and omit to record and analyse what happens. It makes no sense in terms of administrative efficiency and, however little intended, it indicates a careless attitude toward human welfare.'

These are noble sentiments which at least intellectually most social workers would echo. Unfortunately the Committee blotted its own copy-book somewhat in that the Report also says (in paragraph 43):

'We were regrettably unable to sound consumer reaction to the services in any systematic way. This was also related to the fact that we made no attempt to organise a research programme as this would have delayed publication perhaps for another year or two.'

The implication of this statement is that it matters less *where* we are going than getting there quickly and it might therefore itself be considered to indicate 'a careless attitude toward human welfare'. The setting up of the unified social services departments represents a major social work experiment of unprecedented proportions, yet not a single pilot study has been carried out. It is devoutly to be hoped that at least systematic attempts will be made, from the outset, to record and analyse what happens.

There is a mildly manic element about many reports stemming from government appointed committees. They do not gloss over current problems as do many manic persons but they do, if one takes them at their face value, excite enthusiasms and promote the belief that heaven is just around the corner, if only their recommendations are implemented. The human factors, particularly human resistances and human motivations, tend to be under-stressed and there is an essentially 'if only' quality about these reports. *If only* we all loved one another the world would be a better place in which to live. *If only* school teachers had the right approach, children would enjoy school and develop their true potential. *If only* the Seebohm recommendations were accepted in the right spirit, client-centred services would be better. Realistically, it has been said that any ideas we might hold about our clients getting a better service from the new unified departments rests upon our hope and our faith and not so far upon any collected evidence, other than evidence of 'opinions'.

Nonetheless, because we are all concerned to obtain better service for our clients, we do need to ensure that our faith and our hope is utilised to bring about a really improved service and here research can and must be allowed to play an important part.

Much of this research will need to be conducted by central government agencies and university departments. Some will doubtless be undertaken by local authorities using a section attached to the Chief Executive and transcending departmental boundaries, but social services departments may need to be cautioned against holding out too much hope that the research that will come from these bodies will be of immediate value to them, or regard such research activity as absolving them from the need to mount their own agency-based research programmes. They cannot be a substitute for social workers knowing their own district, their own agency and their own clientele. Moreover, local research needs to be an on-going process, and centrally administered ad hoc studies cannot meet this need.

It will certainly be sensible to utilise to the full anything that the central government and other outside research bodies have to offer and to encourage co-operative research with other local authority departments. But in the last analysis, it is the agency itself that is responsible for being knowledgeable about its own area of work and if no other organisation provides the necessary information then the agency must.

What any local authority might do in an inter-departmental structure by way of research may also be of great benefit, particularly in providing background demographic data, and there will plainly be a need for any departmental research unit to work in close association with the inter-departmental unit, drawing upon its expertise and its resources and also contributing to them.

There are three main areas of knowledge that are pertinent to agency-based research:

1. Knowledge concerning the district in which the agency has a responsibility for providing services;
2. Knowledge concerning the existing and potential clientele; and
3. Knowledge concerning the agency itself, its staff, its inter-relationships, its workload, its functioning, the effectiveness of its procedures, etc.

If the Department is to be more than the provider of an unmeasured service and take seriously the idea of promoting social welfare, community involvement and so on, or even if it wants to perform its existing functions more effectively, then it must *know* its district.

The sources of existing social data are widely scattered but the drawing together of this information can fairly easily be undertaken by a member of the department's staff. The Registrar General provides information broken down by local wards in relation to the population by age, sex, marital status, ethnic background, type of housing, density of population per room and in relation to certain domestic facilities.

The local office of the Department of Employment and Productivity has information from which unemployment rates both for the able-bodied and the disabled and for men and women can be calculated. This information may be made available on request by a department of social services and then plotted by ward. Youth Employment Bureaux have similar figures concerning young people.

The Department of Health and Social Security has lists of recipients of social security payments and those who are receiving supplementary benefits so that, with their co-operation, the picture of poverty by ward area can be ascertained. The Registrar of Marriages, Births and Deaths has information concerning infant mortality and other deaths, marriages and births which also might be made available in certain circumstances.

Within the local authority itself the Medical Officer of

Health has considerable information concerning the incidence of disease and the causes of death which can be calculated on a ward basis; the Education Department has knowledge concerning the incidence of truancy, the utilisation of school meals, youth facilities and youth club attendance; and the Housing Departments have more detailed knowledge than the Registrar General on certain characteristics of the state of housing and housing needs, for their districts.

The Post Office and the Electricity Department will have knowledge of vandalism in the district in relation to smashed public telephones, street lighting, etc. The Magistrates Court will have information concerning the pattern of local crime and delinquency.

If this information can be garnered and put together in a way outlined by McCulloch and Philip (389) and McCulloch and Brown (363) for example, then quite a lot can be known about the wards of the district for which the Department of Social Services is responsible. To it, of course, can be added information that exists within the Social Services Department and any other information that it seeks to collect.

The Department should seek to be knowledgeable about the social problems in its district and should have an appreciation of the relationships between social variables, not only in so far as they might be available on a national basis, but, particularly, in relation to its own specific district. What, for example, is the relationship between working mothers and child neglect? Between immigrant groups and family break-up? Between mixed marriages and requests for children to be received into care? Between over-crowding and requests for residential placements for the aged? What characterises the different wards of the district? The answers to these and dozens of similar questions may need to be sought by the Social Services Department. When specialist advice of a social nature is sought, is the agency the first to be consulted? And do we have concrete knowledge when asked, or have to reply from 'impression' or 'opinion'?

In relation to our clientele, while we must necessarily lean heavily upon the findings of psychologists and sociologists, there is likely to be much that is specific to our own district that only the Department is likely to be familiar with. What are the particular characteristics of those who seek our services? What elements are associated with continuing demands for service, or for clients prematurely terminating contact with the Department? What additional provisions would be useful in preventing certain aspects of social pathology and malfunctioning in our districts? What are the advantages and disadvantages of office interviewing and for which types of client? What part might group work play in the counselling of foster-mothers? What frequency of contact makes for successful outcome and for which types of clients? In what areas of activity can volunteers be more effective than professional social workers? And so on. Agency-based research can help to provide the answers to such questions if only someone who has the authority will ask them and set in motion a data-collecting and analysing process.

In seeking to understand our own department better there must be a preparedness to bring any system or activity under examination in order to study its appropriateness and effectiveness. Research can make a contribution to such questions as the number of functions that should be given to any one worker, the optimum caseload size, the appropriate weighting of cases, the factors involved in staff turnover, and many other problems of this kind.

Agencies usually seek to justify their ignorance about their district, their clientele and their own functioning by pointing to their lack of time or competence. Perhaps agencies need to make the time by specifically allocating resources for this very important work and if research competence is lacking then staff must either be specially appointed or given training, (either within the agency or by attendance on specialist courses outside). Much resistance to agency-based research is emotional rather than rational and while social work administrators need to be sensitive to emotional factors affecting their staff, emotions of this kind must not be allowed to hinder the unified department from fulfilling a most important obligation.

While an occasional worker may attempt a small, isolated piece of research, systematic agency-based research comes into being when a conscious and effective decision is made that there shall be a research unit within the Department and the funds are made available to provide and maintain the necessary staff and equipment.

Bearing in mind the need for some balance within the sequence from the existence of human need to the giving of service, a firm decision needs to be arrived at in relation to the extent of expenditure on agency-based research, as compared with the amount of financial resources allocated to other departmental activities. Currently, for most agencies, the amount spent on research is nil and in the beginning stages of the unified department a decision to allocate a definite proportion of the total budget or a definite sum of money for this purpose would seem to be a reasonable one. Unless a deliberate decision is taken along these lines, research will always be last in the queue for a share in scarce resources, whereas if it were regarded as a necessary investment the outcome might well be a better and more effective allocation of those resources in the future, because the allocation would be a more 'informed' one. Large departments may be able to allocate quite substantial resources for research purposes, smaller departments may be unable to do more than set one social worker aside for one day a week; nonetheless, even this would be better than nothing.

The research team might be given the responsibility for collecting, collating and presenting the data required by central government departments, by the local authority and by the social services department itself; for carrying out research projects as directed by the management team; for posing research questions for consideration by the management team; for assisting individual workers within the department who wished to undertake small studies of interest to them; for co-operating with other researchers both within and outside the local authority (including universities); for helping workers to see the value of (and to utilise) research findings; and, with the approval of the Director, for making the findings of their studies available to interested persons.

As agency-based research will be a continuing function of the department, it follows that the relationship between the researchers and other members of the department will be an ongoing one. It is particularly important, therefore, that the concepts of participation and mutual trust be acted upon in a genuine way. While no activity need be exempt from research examination, the close relationship that researchers must of necessity have with the management team may make them suspect as far as many of the staff are concerned. They must therefore be able to assure all staff that no research findings will identify any single individual in a derogatory way and on no account be used to evaluate the work or competence of any individual. Although it might be appropriate for them to assist in developing a staff evaluation schedule, for example, any application of it by them upon individuals would need to be solely for the purpose of evaluating the instrument, and no findings concerning individual members of staff would be communicated to any senior officer.

The use to which a staff evaluation schedule might be put after it had been validated would then lie with the supervisory staff and not with the research unit. It is a sine qua non that the code of ethical practice relevant to the social work profession must apply equally to any researcher in social work.

While centrally based computers within local authorities can play a very valuable role in many areas of work, in practice, agency-based researchers are likely to find considerable drawbacks in using them. One major difficulty is that the needs of other departments are often given higher priority because they are related to the work (as distinct from the research work) of the authority. Ad hoc agency-based research within the social services department may be fortunate to be allocated one hour a week of computer time. As the research unit may not wish to utilise the computer at all for weeks at a time and then require ten hours at one session, real difficulties can be experienced. Neither do large computers readily lend themselves to following through on a spontaneous idea. As research is an art as well as a science, the acting upon hunches or sudden flashes of inspiration needs to be facilitated. The social work researcher in a Social Services Department is therefore likely to find that a desk computer which is readily available to him is far more valuable than computer facilities elsewhere. Where the number of cases or individuals to be studied does not exceed about three hundred, some quite sophisticated work can be done with a system of hand-sorting punched-cards. Alternatively new and second hand punched-card (punching, sorting and counting) equipment is currently on the market and can be bought relatively cheaply.

A 'Seebohm' Bibliography

Robert Foren, Malcolm Brown and Margaret Allen
(University of Bradford)

THE bibliography is divided into a number of sections, viz. Government Publications, Books and Pamphlets, Journal Articles, and Comment and Opinion. Government Publications are arranged by issuing body, Books and Pamphlets by author (with a note of the existence of a bibliography where this is substantial), and Journal Articles and Comment and Opinion by title. The final date for inclusion of an item in the bibliography is 31st October, 1970.

Each work listed has been given code numbers indicating the main fields with which it deals. The categories are as follows.

1. Adoption	17. Law
2. Casework	18. Management and Administration
3. Child Care	19. Maternity and Child Welfare
4. Child Needs and Child Development	20. Medical Social Work
5. Comment and Opinion	21. Mental Health
6. Community Care	22. Moral Welfare
7. Community Work	23. Problem Families
8. Day Care	24. Psychiatric Social Work
9. Education and Education Welfare	25. Reference
10. Elderly	26. Research
11. Handicap (Physical)	27. Research Method
12. Health Service	28. Residential Provision
13. Home Helps	29. Social Policy and Administration
14. Housing	30. Training
15. Immigrants	31. Voluntary Organisations
16. Juvenile Delinquency	

A. GOVERNMENT PUBLICATIONS

1. *Statutes*

1. Children and Young Persons Act, 1933. 23 and 24 Geo. 5 Chapter 12. **3, 16, 17, 28.**
2. National Health Service Act, 1946. 9 and 10 Geo. 6 Chapter 81. **13, 17, 19.**
3. National Assistance Act, 1948. 11 and 12 Geo. 6 Chapter 29. **10, 11, 17, 28, 31.**
4. Children Act, 1948. 11 and 12 Geo. 6 Chapter 43. **3, 17, 28, 31.**
5. Nurseries and Child-Minders Regulation Act, 1948. 11 and 12 Geo. 6 Chapter 53. **3, 8.**
6. Adoption Act, 1958. 7 and 8 Eliz. 2 Chapter 5. **3, 17, 22.**
7. Disabled Persons (Employment) Act, 1958. 6 and 7 Eliz. 2 Chapter 33. **11, 17.**

8. Children Act, 1958. 6 and 7 Eliz. 2 Chapter 65. **3, 17.**
9. Mental Health Act, 1959. 7 and 8 Eliz. 2 Chapter 72. **3, 6, 17, 21, 28.**
10. Matrimonial Proceedings (Magistrates Courts) Act, 1960. 8 and 9 Eliz. 2 Chapter 48. **3, 17.**
11. Mental Health (Scotland) Act, 1960. 8 and 9 Eliz. 2 Chapter 61. **17, 21.**
12. Health Visiting and Social Work (Training) Act, 1962. 10 and 11 Eliz. 2 Chapter 33. **17, 26.**
13. Children and Young Persons Act, 1963. Eliz. 2 1963 Chapter 37. **3, 16, 17.**
14. Matrimonial Causes Act, 1965. Eliz. 2 1965 Chapter 72. **3, 17.**
15. Health Services and Public Health Act, 1968. Eliz. 2 1968 Chapter 46. **6, 10, 13, 17.**
16. Social Work (Scotland) Act, 1968. Eliz. 2 1968 Chapter 49. **3, 17.**
17. Family Law Reform Act, 1969. Eliz. 2 1969 Chapter 46. **3, 17.**
18. Children and Young Persons Act, 1969. Eliz. 2 1969 Chapter 54. **3, 16, 17, 28.**
19. Chronically Sick and Disabled Persons Act, 1970. Eliz. 2 1970 Chapter 44. **11, 17.**
20. Local Authority Social Services Act, 1970. Eliz. 2 1970 Chapter 42.

2. Other Government Publications
21. Central Office of Information (1967) *Children in Britain.* Reference Pamphlet, 34, H.M.S.O. London. **3.**
22. Central Office of Information (1968) *Health Services in Britain.* Reference Pamphlet 20, H.M.S.O. London. **12.**
23. Central Office of Information (1969) *A Guide to Voluntary Service.* H.M.S.O. London. **31.**
24. Centre for Administrative Studies (1967) *Flow Charts, Logical Trees and Algorithms for Rules and Regulations.* By B.N. Lewis, I.S. Horabin and C.P. Gane, CAS Occasional Paper, 2, H.M.S.O. London. **18, 30.**
25. Centre for Administrative Studies (1967) *Network Analysis in Forming a New Organisation.* By W.S. Ryan, CAS Occasional Paper, 3, H.M.S.O. London. **18.**
26. Centre for Administrative Studies (1969) *Management by Objectives in the Civil Service.* By J. Garrett and S.D. Walker, CAS Occasional Paper, 10, H.M.S.O. London. **18.**
27. Department of Education and Science (1966) *Circular 9/66. Co-ordination of Education, Health and Welfare Services for Handicapped Children and Young Persons.* **11**
28. Department of Education and Science (1969) *List of Special Schools for Handicapped Pupils in England and Wales.* List 42, H.M.S.O. London. **3, 11, 25.**
29. Department of Employment and Productivity (1969) *Improving Skills in Working with People: the T-Group.* By P.B. Smith, Training Information Paper, 4, H.M.S.O. London. **30.**
30. Department of Health and Social Security (1968) *The Administrative Structure of the Medical and Related Services in England and Wales.* H.M.S.O. London. **12.**
31. Department of Health and Social Security (1969-) *Annual Report* 1968: Cmnd. 4100
1969: Cmnd. 4462
(Previously issued by Ministry of Health, q.v.). **12.**
32. Department of Health and Social Security (1969) *People with Epilepsy.* Report of a Joint Sub-Committee of the Standing Medical Advisory Committee and the Advisory Committee on the Health and Welfare of Handicapped Persons. H.M.S.O. London. **11.**

33. Department of Health and Social Security (1970) *The Facilities and Services of Psychiatric Hospitals in England and Wales, 1969.* Statistical Report Series, 10, H.M.S.O. London. **21.**

34. Department of Health and Social Security (1970) *National Health Service - The Future Structure of the National Health Service* (Green Paper). H.M.S.O. London. **12, 29.**

35. Department of Health and Social Security (1970) *Psychiatric Hospitals and Units in England and Wales. In-Patient Statistics from the Mental Health Enquiry for the Year 1968.* Statistical Report Series, 11, H.M.S.O. London. **21.**

36. Government Social Survey (1961) *Staffing of Local Authority Residential Homes for Children.* H.M.S.O. London. **3, 28.**

37. Government Social Survey (1968) *Social Welfare for the Elderly* (Two volumes). A study in Thirteen Local Authority Areas in England, Wales and Scotland. By Amelia L. Harris, H.M.S.O. London. **10, 26.**

38. Government Social Survey (1970) *The Home Help Service in England and Wales.* A Survey carried out in 1967 by the Government Social Survey for the Ministry of Health. By Audrey Hunt. H.M.S.O. London. **13, 26.**

39. Home Office (1946) *Report of the Care of Children Committee* (Curtis Committee) Cmd. 6922. (A joint publication of the Home Office, Ministry of Health and Ministry of Education). H.M.S.O. London. **3, 16, 28, 29.**

40. Home Office (1948) *Circular No. 160/1948, Children Act, 1948.* **3, 17.**

41. Home Office (1951-   )
    6th Report on the Work of the Children's Department (1951)
    7th Report on the Work of the Children's Department (1955)
    Report on the Work of the Children's Department, 1955-60. (1961)
    Report on the Work of the Children's Department, 1961-63. H.C.155 (1964)
    Report on the Work of the Children's Department, 1964-66. H.C.603 (1967)
    Report on the Work of the Children's Department, 1967-69. H.C.140 (1970)
    H.M.S.O. London. **3, 16, 28.**

42. Home Office (1955) *Memorandum for the Guidance of Managers and Staff of Approved Schools, and of Persons Appointed by Managers to Supervise on their Behalf, Boys and Girls Released from Approved Schools.* **3, 16, 28.**

43. Home Office (1955) *Memorandum on the Boarding-Out of Children Regulations.* H.M.S.O. London. **3, 17.**

44. Home Office (1960) *Circular No. 156/1960, The Mental Health Act, 1959.* **17, 21, 28.**

45. Home Office (1960) *Report of the Committee on Children and Young Persons* (Ingleby Committee). Cmnd. 1191. H.M.S.O. London. **3, 16, 28.**

46. Home Office (1963) *Circular No. 204/1963, Section 1 of the Children and Young Persons Act, 1963.* **3, 17.**

47. Home Office (1964) *Circular No. 15/1964, Children and Young Persons Act, 1963.* **3, 16, 28.**

48. Home Office (1964) *Circular No. 17/1964 and 22/1964, Children and Young Persons Act, 1963 – Parts I and III.* **3, 17.**

49. Home Office (1964) *Needs of Young Children in Care.* H.M.S.O. London. **3.**

50. Home Office (1965) *The Child, the Family and the Young Offender.* Cmnd. 2742. H.M.S.O. London. **16, 29.**

51. Home Office (1965) *Circular No. 102/1965, Section I of the Children and Young Persons Act, 1963 – Reports to the Secretary of State.* **3, 29, 31.**

52. Home Office (1965) *Directory of Approved Schools, Remand Homes and Special Reception Centres in England and Wales.* H.M.S.O. London. **25.**

53. Home Office (1966) *Circular No. 134/1966, Medical Examination of Children in Care.* **3.**

54. Home Office (1966) *Joint Circular* (with Welsh Board of Health and Welsh

Office) *178(W)/1966, Homeless Families – Temporary Accommodation.* **3, 14, 23.**

55. Home Office (1967) *Circular No. 64/1967, Residential Child Care Staff – National Pattern for In-Service Study Courses.* **28, 30.**

56. Home Office (1967) *Juvenile Offenders and Those in Need of Care, Protection or Control (England and Wales).* **3, 16, 28.**

57. Home Office (1968) *Children in Trouble,* Cmnd. 3601. H.M.S.O. London. **3, 16, 28, 29, 31.**

58. Home Office (1969) *Ancillary Staff in Children's Departments.* By Patricia Lowry. A Home Office Research Unit Report. **3, 18, 26.**

59. Home Office (1969) *Children Act, 1948 – Summary of Local Authorities' Returns of Children in Care at 31st March, 1969* (Issued by the Home Office Statistical Division). **3, 28, 31.**

60. Home Office (1969) *Circular No. 254/1969, Children and Young Persons Act, 1969* (Timetable for bringing Act into force). **3, 17.**

61. Home Office (1969) *Circular No. 261/1969, Children and Young Persons Act, 1969 – Foster Children.* **3.**

62. Home Office (1969) *Workloads in Children's Departments.* By Eleanor Grey. A Home Office Research Unit Report. H.M.S.O. London. **3, 18, 26, 29.**

63. Home Office (1970) *Adoption of Children.* Working Paper Containing the Provisional Proposals of the Departmental Committee on the Adoption of Children (Chairman: Sir W. Houghton). H.M.S.O. London. **1, 3, 29.**

64. Home Office (1970) *Children in Care in England and Wales* – Particulars of the number of children in care of local authorities under the Children Act, 1948, the manner of their accommodation, and the estimated costs of maintenance; and the number of children in registered voluntary homes or boarded out by voluntary organisations. Published annually: latest (1969) Cmnd. 4263. H.M.S.O. London. **3, 28, 31.**

65. Home Office (1970) *Circular No. 44/1970, Children and Young Persons Act, 1969 – Establishment of Children's Regional Planning Committees.* **18, 28, 29.**

66. Home Office (1970) *First Report of the Study Group on Fieldwork Training* (Issued by the Central Training Council in Child Care, Committee 'A'). **3, 30.**

67. Home Office (1970) *A Guide to Adoption Practice* (Chairman: T.F. Tucker). Advisory Councils on Child Care for England and Wales and for Scotland. Publication, 2. H.M.S.O. London. **1, 3, 17.**

68. Home Office (1970) *Part I of the Children and Young Persons Act, 1969. A Guide for Courts and Practitioners.* H.M.S.O. London. **3, 17.**

69. Home Office (1970) *Playgroups – the Development of Dual Purpose Groups in Social Work Education* (Issued by the Central Training Council in Child Care). **7, 30.**

70. Home Office (1970) *The Residential Placement in the Training of Social Workers* (Issued by the Central Training Council in Child Care). **3, 28, 30.**

71. Home Office (1970) *Short Courses for Staff of the Child Care Services, 1970-71* (Issued by the Central Training Council in Child Care). **3, 28, 30.**

72. Home Office (1970) *Staff Development and In-Service Study for the Staff of Children's Departments* (Issued by the Central Training Council in Child Care). **3, 18, 30.**

73. Home Office (1970) *Statistics Relating to Approved Schools, Remand Homes and Attendance Centres in England and Wales for the Year 1969.* Published annually: latest (1969) H.C. 144. H.M.S.O. London. **16, 28.**

74. Home Office (1970) *The Structure of Courses – Some Implications for the Patterns of Fieldwork Training* (Issued by the Central Training Council in Child Care). **3, 30.**

75. House of Commons (1970) Parliamentary Debates (Hansard), Vol. 796, No. 68, 26th February, 1970, Cols. 1406-1520. *Debate on Second Reading of the Local Authority Social Services Bill.* H.M.S.O. London. **17, 29.**

76. Interdepartmental Social Work Group (Department of Health and Social Security, Home Office, Welsh Office) (1970) *Circular 1/70, Local Authority Social Services Act, 1970.* **17.**

77. Interdepartmental Social Work Group (Department of Health and Social Security, Home Office, Welsh Office) (1970) *Circular 2/70, Local Authority Social Services Act, 1970. The Local Authority Social Services Act, 1970 (Commencement No. 1) Order 1970 (S.I. 1970, No. 1143 (C.29)).* **17.**

78. Ministry of Education (1955) *Report of the Committee on Maladjusted Children* (Underwood Report). H.M.S.O. London. **3, 21, 28, 29.**

79. Ministry of Health (1948) *Circular 143/48, Standards for Day Nurseries.* **8.**

80. Ministry of Health (1951) *Report of the Committee on Social Workers in the Mental Health Services* (The Mackintosh Committee). Cmd. 8260. H.M.S.O. London. **21, 29.**

81. Ministry of Health (1959) *Report of the Working Party on Social Workers in the Local Authority Health and Welfare Services* (The Younghusband Report). **10, 11, 13, 19, 21, 29, 30.**

82. Ministry of Health (1961-68) *Annual Report*

1960: Part I Health and Welfare Services	Cmnd. 1418
1961: Part I Health and Welfare Services	Cmnd. 1754
1962: Health and Welfare Services	Cmnd. 2062
1963: Health and Welfare Services	Cmnd. 2389
1964: Annual Report of the Ministry of Health	Cmnd. 2688
1965: Annual Report of the Ministry of Health	Cmnd. 3039
1966: Annual Report of the Ministry of Health	Cmnd. 3326
1967: Annual Report of the Ministry of Health	Cmnd. 3702

    1968: *See* Department of Health and Social Security. **12.**

83. Ministry of Health (1962) *A Hospital Plan for England and Wales.* H.M.S.O. London. **6. 12.**

84. Ministry of Health (1962) *Residential Accommodation for Elderly People.* Local Authority Building Note, 2. H.M.S.O. London. **10.**

85. Ministry of Health (1962) *The Training of Staff of Training Centres for the Mentally Sub-Normal* (Report of a Sub-Committee of the Standing Mental Health Advisory Committee, Central Health Services Council – The Scott Report). H.M.S.O. London. **21, 30.**

86. Ministry of Health (1963) *Health and Welfare – The Development of Community Care* (Plans for the Health and Welfare Services of the Local Authorities in England and Wales). Cmnd. 1973. H.M.S.O. London. **6.**

87. Ministry of Health (1964) *Health and Welfare: The Development of Community Care.* Revision to 1973-74 of Plans for the Health and Welfare Services of the Local Authorities in England and Wales. H.M.S.O. London. **6.**

88. Ministry of Health (1966) *Health and Welfare: The Development of Community Care.* Revision to 1975-76 of Plans for the Health and Welfare Services of the Local Authorities in England and Wales. Cmnd. 3022. H.M.S.O. London. **6.**

89. Ministry of Health (1967) *Residential Hostels for the Mentally Disordered,* Local Authority Building Note, 6. H.M.S.O. London. **21.**

90. Ministry of Health (1968) *Circular 36/68, Health Services and Public Health Act, 1968, Section 68* (Amendment to the Mental Health Act, 1959). **21.**

91. Ministry of Health (1968) *Circular 37/68, Day Care Facilities for Children under Five.* **3, 8.**

92. Ministry of Housing and Local Government (1961) *Circular No. 10/61, Services for Old People: Co-operation between Housing, Local Health and Welfare Authorities and Voluntary Organisations.* **10, 31.**

93. Ministry of Housing and Local Government (1964) *Circular No. 54/64, Flats for the Disabled.* **11.**

94. Ministry of Housing and Local Government (1965) *The First Hundred Families: a Guide to the Community Services and Facilities which should be available for the First Families arriving in an Expanding Town* (Report of a Study Group of the Central Housing Advisory Committee.) H.M.S.O. London. **7.**

95. Ministry of Housing and Local Government (1967) *Local Government Administration in England and Wales.* By Margaret Harrison and Alan Norton (An Enquiry carried out for the Committee on the Management of Local Government (Chairman: J. Maud), Management of Local Government, vol. 5). H.M.S.O. London. **3, 14, 18, 29.**

96. Ministry of Housing and Local Government (1967) *Staffing of Local Government.* Report of the (Mallaby) Committee on the Staffing of Local Government. H.M.S.O. London. **18.**

97. Ministry of Housing and Local Government (1968) *Report of the Committee on Local Authority and Allied Personal Social Services* (Seebohm Report). Cmnd. 3703. H.M.S.O. London. **3, 6, 10, 11, 13, 14, 18, 21, 26, 29, 30.**

98. Ministry of Housing and Local Government (1969) *Circular 82/69, Accommodation Specially Designed for Old People.* H.M.S.O. London. **10.**

99. Ministry of Housing and Local Government (1969) *Grouped Flatlets for Old People - A Sociological Study,* Design Bulletin, 2. H.M.S.O. London. **10.**

100. Ministry of Housing and Local Government (1969) *Some Aspects of Designing for Old People.* Design Bulletin, 1. H.M.S.O. London. **10.**

101. Ministry of Housing and Local Government (1970) *Reform of Local Government in England.* Cmnd. 4276. H.M.S.O. London. **29.**

102. Ministry of Labour (2nd ed. 1961) *Services for the Disabled - An Account of the Services Provided for the Disabled by Government Departments, Local Authorities and Voluntary Organisations in the U.K.* (Report of the Standing Committee on the Rehabilitation and Resettlement of Disabled Persons). H.M.S.O. London. **11, 31.**

103. Ministry of Pensions and National Insurance (1966) *Financial and Other Circumstances of Retirement Pensioners.* H.M.S.O. London. **10.**

104. Royal Commission on Local Government in England 1966-69 (1969) (Redcliffe–Maud Report) Vol. 1. *Report.* Cmnd. 4040. **18, 29.**

105. Royal Commission on Local Government in England 1966-69 (1969) (Redcliffe-Maud Report) Vol. III *Research Appendices.* Cmnd. 4040-II. H.M.S.O. London (Especially Appendix 12: *Home Office - The Children's Service).* **3, 26, 29**

106. *Royal Commission on Local Government in England 1966-69* (1968) *Local Authority Services and the Characteristics of Administrative Areas.* By M. Woolf. Research Studies, 5. H.M.S.O. London. **18, 29.**

107. Scottish Education Department (1970) *Handicapped Children in Care of Local Authorities and Voluntary Organisations* (Report of the Committee appointed by the Scottish Advisory Committee on Child Care - the Mitchell Report). H.M.S.O. Edinburgh. **3, 11, 29.**

108. Scottish Home and Health Department (1964) *Children and Young Persons (Scotland)* (The Kilbrandon Report). Cmnd. 2306. H.M.S.O. London. **3, 16, 18.**

109. Scottish Home and Health Department (1966) *Social Work and the Community. Proposals for Reorganising Local Authority Services in Scotland.* Cmnd. 3065. H.M.S.O. London.

110. Scottish Home and Health Department (1970) *No Folks of Their Own - A Report on One Aspect of Community Care of the Mentally Handicapped*

(The McDonald Report) (Issued by the Mental Welfare Commission for Scotland). H.M.S.O. Edinburgh. **6, 21.**
111. Scottish Home and Health Department (1970) *Services for the Elderly with Mental Disorder* (Report of a Sub-Committee of the Standing Medical Advisory Committee, Scottish Health Services Council – The Millar Report). H.M.S.O. Edinburgh. **6, 10, 21, 29.**
112. Statutory Instrument (1955) No. 1377 *The Boarding-Out of Children Regulations, 1955.* H.M.S.O. London. **3, 17.**
113. Statutory Instrument (1970) No. 1143 (C.29) *The Local Authority Social Services Act, 1970 (Commencement No. 1) Order 1970.* H.M.S.O. London. **17.**

B. BOOKS AND PAMPHLETS

114. Adams, M. (ed.) (1960) *The Mentally Subnormal: The Social Casework Approach,* Heinemann, London (Bibliography). **2, 21.**
115. Agate, J. and Meacher, M. (1969) *The Care of the Old,* Fabian Research Series, 278 Fabian Society, London. **10.**
116. Association of Child Care Officers (1969) *Working Party on Professional Integrity in the Child Care Service – Report.* London. **3, 29.**
117. Association of Children's Officers (1968) *Report of an Inquiry into Boarding-Out.* Trowbridge, Wilts. **3.**
118. Association of Municipal Corporations *and* County Councils Association (1966) *Proceedings of Child Care Conference, Hastings, April, 1966,* London. **3.**
119. Association of Municipal Corporations *and* County Councils Association (1969) *'Seebohm Report' Study Conference, London, 1968.* London. **5.**
120. Association of Social Workers (1966) *New Thinking about Administration.* London. **18.**
121. Banwell, L.G. (7th edition 1967, with supplements) *Clarke Hall and Morrison's Law Relating to Children and Young Persons,* Butterworth, London. **17.**
122. Beedell, Christopher (1970) *Residential Life with Children,* Routledge & Kegan Paul, London (Bibliography). **3, 28, 30.**
123. Biestek, Felix P. (New edition 1967) *The Casework Relationship,* Unwin University Books, London. **2.**
124. Blau, Peter and Scott, W. Richard (1963) *Formal Organizations – A Comparative Approach,* Routledge & Kegan Paul, London (Bibliography). **18.**
125. Boss, Peter (1967) *Social Policy and the Young Delinquent,* Routledge & Kegan Paul, London (Bibliography). **3, 16, 28, 29.**
126. Brill, K.H. (1962) *Children – Not Cases: Social Work for Children and Their Families,* National Children's Home, London. **3, 28.**
127. Brill, K.H. and Thomas, R. (1964) *Children in Homes,* Gollancz, London (Bibliography). **3, 28.**
128. British Psychological Society (1968) *Memorandum on the Seebohm Report* London. **9, 21.**
129. Bromley, P.M. (3rd edition 1966 with 1969 supplement) *Family Law,* Butterworth, London. **17.**
130. Brown, S. Clement and Gloyne, E.R. (1966) *The Field Training of Social Workers,* George Allen & Unwin, London. **30.**
131. Brown, Wilfred (1965) *Exploration in Management,* Penguin Books, Harmondsworth. **18.**
132. Bruce, Maurice. (4th edition 1968) *The Coming of the Welfare State,* B. T. Batsford, London. **29.**

133. Burton, Lindy. (1968) *Vulnerable Children,* Routledge & Kegan Paul, London. 3.
134. Butrym, Zofia. (1967) *Social Work in Medical Care,* Routledge & Kegan Paul, London (Bibliography). 6, 20.
135. Butrym, Zofia. (1968) *Medical Social Work in Action,* G. Bell and Sons, London. 12, 18, 20, 26.
136. Calouste Gulbenkian Foundation Study Group on Training (1969) *Community Work and Social Charge,* Longmans, Green & Co., London. 7, 30.
137. Caplan, Gerald. (1961) *An Approach to Community Mental Health,* Tavistock Publications, London. 6, 21.
138. Caplow, Theodore. (1964) *Principles of Organization,* Harcourt, Brace and World, New York. 18.
139. Carlebach, Julius. (1970) *Caring for Children in Trouble,* Routledge & Kegan Paul, London. 16, 28, 29.
140. Clarke, Raymond T. (1963) *Working with Communities,* National Council of Social Service, London (Bibliography). 6, 31.
141. Conference of Principal Probation and After-Care Officers (1968) *Observations on the White Paper 'Children in Trouble'.* 16.
142. Cooper, Joan D. (1965) *The Role of Social Work - Administration and Practice (in* Kellmer-Pringle, M.L.(ed.) *Investment in Children),* Longmans, Green & Co., London. 3.
143. Council for Children's Welfare (1965) *A Family Service and a Family Court,* London. 16, 18.
144. Council for Children's Welfare and the Fisher Group (1958) *Families with Problems* (Some Proposals for a Family Service and for changes in Juvenile Court Procedure based on evidence submitted to the Ingleby Committee). London. 16, 29.
145. Council for Training in Social Work (1967) *Staff Development in Social Work,* Discussion Paper, 1, London. 30.
146. Daniel, G.R. and Freeman, H.C. (eds) (1968) *Treatment of Mental Disorders in the Community,* Baillière, Tindall and Cassell, London. 6, 21.
147. Davies, B. (1968) *Social Needs and Resources in Local Services: A Study of Variations in Standards of Provision of Personal Social Services between Local Authority Areas,* Michael Joseph, London. 18.
148. Denney, Anthony. (1966) *Children in Need,* S.C.M. Press, London (Bibliography). 3.
149. De Schweinitz, Elizabeth and Karl (1962) *Interviewing in the Social Services,* National Council of Social Service, London. 2.
150. Dinnage, Rosemary and Kellmer-Pringle, M.L. (1967) *Foster Home Care - Facts and Fallacies - A Review of Research in the U.S.A., Western Europe, Israel and Great Britain, 1944-1966,* Longmans, Green & Co., London. (Bibliography). 3, 26.
151. Dinnage, Rosemary and Kellmer-Pringle, M.L. (1967) *Residential Child Care - Facts and Fallacies,* Longmans, Green & Co., London. (Bibliography). 3, 26, 28.
152. Donnison, D.V. (1962) *The Ingleby Report - Three Critical Essays,* Fabian Research Series, 231 Fabian Society, London. 6, 16, 29.
153. Donnison, D.V. and Chapman, Valierie *et al.* (1965) *Social Policy and Administration - Studies in the Development of Social Services at the Local Level,* George Allen & Unwin, London (Bibliography). 3, 13, 18, 29.
154. Drain, G. (1966) *The Organisation and Practice of Local Government* (especially Chapter 7-Health, Welfare and Children), Heinemann, London. 29.
155. Drucker, Peter F. (1964) *Managing for Results,* Heinemann, London. 18.
156. Drucker, Peter F. (1967) *The Effective Executive,* Heinemann, London. 18.
157. Edwards, A.H. (3rd Edition 1961) *Mental Health Services,* Shaw, London. 21.

Appendix: Bibliography

158. Etzioni, Amitai. (1964) *Modern Organizations,* Prentice-Hall, Englewood Cliffs, New Jersey. **18.**

159. Etzioni, Amitai (ed.) (1969) *The Semi-Professions and their Organization,* The Free Press, New York. **18.**

160. Eyden, J.L.M. (1969) *Social Policy in Action,* Routledge & Kegan Paul, London. **29.**

161. Fabian Society (1970) *The Fifth Social Service: a Critical Analysis of the Seebohm Proposals.* By Peter Townsend *et al.* Fabian Society, London. **5.**

162. Family Welfare Association (1970) *Charities Digest, 1970,* Family Welfare Association and Butterworth, London. **25.**

163. Family Welfare Association (1970) *Guide to the Social Services* (Revised Annually), London (Bibliography). **25.**

164. Fanshel, David. (ed.) (1962) *Research in Social Welfare Administration,* National Association of Social Workers, New York. **18, 26.**

165. Farndale, J. (1961) *The Day Hospital Movement in Great Britain: An Analysis and Description of 65 Day Hospitals and Day Centres with Special Reference to Psychiatric and Geriatric Day Hospitals Visited in 1958-9,* Pergamon Press, Oxford (Bibliography). **6, 10, 21.**

166. Farndale, J. (ed.) (1965) *Trends in Social Welfare,* Pergamon Press, Oxford. **10, 11, 14, 21, 22, 28, 29.**

167. Ferard, Margaret L. and Hunnybun, Noel K. (1962) *The Caseworker's Use of Relationships,* Tavistock Publications, London. **2.**

168. Forder, Anthony. (1966) *Social Casework and Administration,* Faber & Faber, London. **2, 3, 18, 29, 31.**

169. Forder, Anthony. (1969) *Penelope Hall's Social Services of England and Wales,* Routledge & Kegan Paul, London. **3, 9, 10, 11, 12, 29.**

170. Foren, Robert and Bailey, Royston. (1968) *Authority in Social Casework,* Pergamon Press, Oxford (Bibliography). **2, 3, 20, 23, 24.**

171. Forman, J.A.S. and Fairbairn, E.M. (1968) *Social Casework in General Practice - A Report on an Experiment Carried Out in a General Practice,* Oxford University Press, London. **2, 6, 12, 20, 26.**

172. Freeman, Hugh and Farndale, James. (eds.) (1963) *Trends in the Mental Health Services,* Pergamon Press, Oxford. **6, 12, 21.**

173. Freud, Anna (revised edition 1968) *The Ego and the Mechanisms of Defence,* Hogarth Press, London. **2, 3, 4, 20, 21, 24.**

174. George, Victor (1970) *Foster Care: Theory and Practice,* Routledge & Kegan Paul, London (Bibliography). **3, 26.**

175. Gibbs, J. (1968) *Patterns of Residential Care for Children,* National Children's Home, London. **3, 28.**

176. Goldberg, E.M. (1966) *Welfare in the Community - Talks on Social Work to Welfare Officers,* National Council of Social Service, London. **2, 11, 21.**

177. Gooch, Stan and Kellmer-Pringle, M.L. (1966) *Four Years On - A Follow-up Study at School Leaving Age of Children Formerly Attending a Traditional and a Progressive Junior School,* Longmans, Green & Co., London (Bibliography). **3, 4, 26.**

178. Goodacre, Iris. (1966) *Adoption Policy and Practice,* George Allen & Unwin, London (Bibliography). **1, 3, 22.**

179. Griffith, J.A.G. (1966) *Central Departments and Local Authorities,* George Allen & Unwin, London. **3, 10, 11, 18, 19, 21, 28, 29.**

180. Grundy, F. (7th edition, revised 1968) *The New Public Health: An Introduction for Midwives, Health Visitors and Social Workers,* Lewis, London. **6, 8, 10, 11, 12, 13, 17, 28.**

181. Guilford, J.P. (4th edition 1965) *Fundamental Statistics in Psychology and Education,* McGraw Hill, New York. **27.**

182. Gunzburg, H.C. (1960) *Social Rehabilitation of the Subnormal,* Baillière, Tindall and Cox, London (Bibliography). **21.**

183. Hall, M. Penelope and Howes, Ismene V. (1965) *The Church in Social Work,* Routledge & Kegan Paul, London. **22, 28, 29, 31.**

184. Halmos, Paul. (1965) *The Faith of the Counsellors,* Constable, London (Bibliography). **2.**

185. Hargrove, A.L. (Revised edition 1963) *The N.A.M.H. Guide to the Mental Health Act, 1959,* National Association for Mental Health, London. **21.**

186. Harris, A.I. (1961) *Meals on Wheels for Old People* A Report of an Inquiry by the Government Social Survey. National Corporation for the Care of Old People, London. **10.**

187. Harvey, A. (1960) *Casualties of the Welfare State,* Fabian Tract, 321. Fabian Society, London. **14.**

188. Heimler, Eugene. (1967) *Mental Illness and Social Work,* Penguin Books, Harmondsworth. **6, 21.**

189. Hersey, P. and Blanchard, K.H. (1969) *Management of Organizational Behavior – Utilizing Human Resources,* Prentice Hall, Englewood Cliffs, New Jersey. **18.**

190. Herzog, Elizabeth. (1959) *Some Guide Lines for Evaluative Research,* U.S. Department of Health, Education and Welfare. Children's Bureau Publication, No. 375 (Bibliography). **27.**

191. Heywood, Jean S. (1964) *An Introduction to Teaching Casework Skills,* Routledge & Kegan Paul, London. **30.**

192. Heywood, Jean S. (2nd edition, revised 1965) *Children in Care,* Routledge & Kegan Paul, London. **3.**

193. Holden, D.A. (1970) *Child Legislation 1969,* Butterworth, London. **3, 16, 17, 28.**

194. Hollis, Florence. (1964) *Casework – A Psycho-Social Therapy,* Random House, New York (Bibliography). **2.**

195. Hunt, A. (1969) *Caring for the Severely Subnormal,* Spastics Society, London. **11.**

196. Institute of Municipal Treasurers and Accountants (1969) *Cost Benefit Analysis in Local Government,* London (Bibliography). **18.**

197. Institute of Municipal Treasurers and Accountants and Society of County Treasurers (1970) *Children Services Statistics* (Annual, 1968/69 latest), London. **25.**

198. Institute of Municipal Treasurers and Accountants and Society of County Treasurers (1970) *Local Health Services Statistics* (Annual, 1968/69 latest), London. **12, 26.**

199. Institute of Municipal Treasurers and Accountants and Society of County Treasurers (1970) *Welfare Services Statistics* (Annual, 1968/69 latest), London. **25.**

200. Irvine, E.E. (ed.) (1967) *Casework and Mental Illness,* Association of Psychiatric Social Workers, London. **2, 21.**

201. Jackson, Stephen. (1966) *Special Education in England and Wales,* Oxford University Press, London (Bibliography). **3, 11, 21, 31.**

202. Jaques, E. (1951) *The Changing Culture of a Factory,* Tavistock Publications, London. **18.**

203. Jefferys, Margot. (1965) *An Anatomy of Social Welfare Services.* A Survey of Social Welfare Staff and their Clients in the County of Buckinghamshire, Michael Joseph, London. **3, 9, 10, 11, 12, 20, 21.**

204. Jehu, Derek. (Undated) *Casework Before Admission to Care,* Association of Child Care Officers (N.W. Region). **2, 3.**

205. Joint University Council for Social and Public Administration (1966) *Fieldwork in Social Administration Courses,* National Council of Social Service, London. **30.**

206. Jones, Kathleen. (1960) *Mental Health and Social Policy (1845-1959),* Routledge & Kegan Paul, London. **17, 21, 29.**

Appendix: Bibliography

207. Jones, Kathleen and Sidebotham, R. (1962) *Mental Hospitals at Work,* Routledge & Kegan Paul, London. **21.**
208. Kahn, Jack H. and Nursten, Jean P. (2nd edition 1968) *Unwillingly to School - School Phobia or School Refusal - A Medico-Social Problem,* Pergamon Press, Oxford (Bibliography). **2, 9, 21, 24.**
209. Kastell, J. (1962) *Casework in Child Care,* Routledge & Kegan Paul, London. **2, 3.**
210. Keith-Lucas, Alan. (1957) *Some Casework Concepts for the Public Welfare Worker,* University of North Carolina Press, Chapel Hill. **2.**
211. Kellmer-Pringle, M.L. (1966) *Adoption - Facts and Fallacies - A Review of Research in the U.S.A., Canada and Great Britain, 1948-1965,* Longmans, Green & Co., London (Bibliography). **1, 3, 22, 26.**
212. Kellmer-Pringle, M.L. *et al.* (1966) *Eleven Thousand Seven-Year-Olds,* Longmans, Green & Co., London. **3, 4, 26.**
213. Kellmer-Pringle, M.L. (1969) *Caring for Children - A Symposium on Co-operation in Child Care,* Longmans, Green & Co., London (Bibliography). **3, 15, 28, 31.**
214. Kent, Bessie. (1969) *Social Work Supervision in Practice,* Pergamon Press, Oxford. **30.**
215. Kershaw, J.D. (2nd edition 1966) *Handicapped Children,* Heinemann, London. **11.**
216. Klein, Josephine. (1965) *Samples from English Cultures* (Vol. 2), Routledge & Kegan Paul, London. **4.**
217. Kornitzer, Margaret. (3rd edition 1970) *Adoption,* Putnam, London (Bibliography). **1, 3.**
218. Lambert, David. (ed.) (1968) *Residential Staff in Child Care,* Annual Review of the Residential Child Care Association, Vol. 16. **3, 28, 30.**
219. Lawrence, P.R. and Lorsch, J.W. (1969) *Developing Organizations - Diagnosis and Action,* Addison-Wesley, Reading, Mass. **18.**
220. Leavitt, H.J. and Pondy, L.R. (eds.) (1964) *Readings in Managerial Psychology,* University of Chicago Press, London. **18.**
221. Leeding, A.E. (1966) *Child Care Manual,* Butterworth, London. **1, 3, 16, 17, 28, 29.**
222. Leissner, Aryeh. (1967) *Family Advice Services - An Exploratory Study of a Sample of Such Services organised by Children's Departments in England,* Longmans, Green & Co., London. **3, 7, 26, 29, 31.**
223. Litterer, Joseph A. (1963) *Organizations: Structure and Behavior.* John Wiley, New York. **18.**
224. London Council of Social Service (1963) *Day Care Service for the Aged and Infirm in their own Homes: Report of an Experiment in St. Pancras from September, 1961 to March, 1963.* National Council of Social Service, London. **8, 10.**
225. London Council of Social Service (1969) *Implications of the Seebohm Report for Voluntary Organisations.* **29, 31.**
226. McGuire, Sheelagh. (1970) *An Analysis of Principal Probation Officers' Annual Reports for 1968* (Unpublished B.A. Dissertation, University of Bradford). **18, 26.**
227. MacRae, Stuart and Page, Stuart. (1966) *Casebook - Studies in Administration,* Edward Arnold, London. **18, 29.**
228. Marsh, David C. (1965) *An Introduction to the Study of Social Administration,* Routledge & Kegan Paul, London. **3, 10, 11, 16, 21, 29, 31.**
229. Martin, F.M. and Rehin, G.F. (1969) *Towards Community Care: Problems and Policies in the Mental Health Service.* P.E.P. Broadsheet, 508, Political and Economic Planning, London. **6, 21.**
230. Miller, E.J. and Rice, A.K. (1967) *Systems of Organisation: the Control of Task and Sentient Boundaries,* Tavistock Publications, London. **18.**

231. Mittler, P. (1966) *The Mental Health Services,* Fabian Research Series, 252, Fabian Society, London. **21.**
232. Mittler, P. (1968) *Mental Health Services in the Community,* Fabian Occasional Paper, 4, Fabian Society, London. **6, 21.**
233. *Municipal Year Book* (1970) Municipal Journal Ltd., London. **25.**
234. Munro, Alistair & McCulloch, Wallace. (1969) *Psychiatry for Social Workers,* Pergamon Press, Oxford. **2, 4, 6, 10, 21.**
235. National Association for Mental Health (1965) *Child Guidance and Child Psychiatry as an Integral Part of Community Services.* London (Bibliography). **6, 21.**
236. National Association for Mental Health (1965) *Directory of Adult Psychiatric Out-Patient Facilities in England, Wales and Scotland, Northern Ireland, the Isle of Man and the Channel Islands, 1964-65.* London. **21, 25.**
237. National Association for Mental Health (1970) *Directory of Child Guidance and School Psychological Services.* London. **21, 25.**
238. National Association of Probation Officers (1968) *Comments on the White Paper: 'Children in Trouble'.* London. **3, 16.**
239. National Bureau for Co-operation in Child Care (1966) *Exploration and Innovation in Child Care: Papers Read at Second Annual Meeting, 1965.* **3.**
240. National Bureau for Co-operation in Child Care (1969) *Directory of Voluntary Organisations Concerned with Children,* Longmans, Green & Co., London. **3, 25, 31.**
241. National Corporation for the Care of Old People (1961) *Outlines of a Survey on the Meals on Wheels Service* (Summary of a Report by the Government Social Survey). London. **10.**
242. National Corporation for the Care of Old People (1963) *Accommodation for the Mentally Infirm Aged: Report.* London. **10.**
243. National Council for the Unmarried Mother and Her Child (1966) *The Unmarried Mother and Her Child in Residential Care: Report of a Conference held 14th May, 1964.* London. **22, 28.**
244. National Council of Social Service (1957) *The Welfare of the Disabled.* London. **11, 21.**
245. National Council of Social Service (1965) *Community Organisation – Work in Progress.* London. **6, 29, 31.**
246. National Council of Social Service (1967) *Caring for People – Staffing Residential Homes – The Report of the Committee of Enquiry* (Williams Report), George Allen & Unwin, London. **3, 10, 11, 26, 28, 30.**
247. National Council of Social Service (1969) *The Volunteer Worker in the Social Services* (Report of a Committee set up by the N.C.S.S. and the N.I.S.W.T., The Aves Report). London. **29, 31.**
248. National Council of Social Service (Revised edition 1970) *Voluntary Social Services: a Handbook of Information and Directory of Organisations.* London. **25, 31.**
249. National Old People's Welfare Council (revised edition 1961) *Statutory and Voluntary Services from which Elderly People may Benefit,* National Council for Social Service, London. **10.**
250. National Old People's Welfare Council (revised edition 1962) *Statutory Provision for Old People.* National Council of Social Service, London (Bibliography). **10.**
251. National Old People's Welfare Council (revised edition 1963) *The Organisation of a Visiting Service by an Old People's Welfare Committee,* National Council of Social Service, London. **10, 31.**
252. National Old People's Welfare Council (revised edition 1965) *Old People's Welfare Committees: Why They Are Needed, How They Are Started, What They Do,* National Council of Social Service, London. **10, 31.**
253. National Old People's Welfare Council (revised edition 1969) *Boarding-Out*

for Elderly People, National Council of Social Service, London (Bibliography). **10.**

254. New Barnett Papers, No. 1. (1964) *The Family in Modern Society,* Oxford University, Department of Social and Administrative Studies. **3, 21, 29.**

255. Nicholson, Jill. (1968) *Mother and Baby Homes - A Survey of Homes for Unmarried Mothers,* George Allen & Unwin, London (Bibliography). **3, 22, 28.**

256. Odiorne, G.S. (1970) *Management by Objectives,* Pitman, London. **18.**

257. Packman, Jean. (1968) *Child Care Needs and Numbers,* George Allen & Unwin, London. **3, 16, 21, 26, 28, 31.**

258. Parfit, Jessie. (ed.) (1967) *The Community's Children - Long-Term Substitute Care: A Guide for the Intelligent Layman,* Longmans, Green & Co., London (Bibliography). **3, 4, 28.**

259. Parker, Julia. (1965) *Local Health and Welfare Services,* George Allen & Unwin, London. **3, 10, 11, 21, 29, 31.**

260. Parker, R.A. (1966) *Decision in Child-Care - A Study of Prediction in Fostering,* George Allen & Unwin, London (Bibliography). **3, 26.**

261. Perlman, Helen Harris. (1957) *Social Casework - A Problem-Solving Process,* University of Chicago Press, Chicago. **2.**

262. Peters, R.J. and Kinnaird, J. (eds.) (1965) *Health Services Administration: A Source Book,* Livingstone, Edinburgh (Bibliography). **12.**

263. Pettes, Dorothy E. (1967) *Supervision in Social Work - A Method of Student Training and Staff Development,* George Allen & Unwin, London (Bibliography). **30.**

264. Philp, A.F. (1963) *Family Failure - A Study of 129 Families with Multiple Problems,* Faber & Faber, London (Bibliography). **23, 26.**

265. Pincus, Lily. (ed.) (1960) *Marriage: Studies in Emotional Conflict and Growth,* Methuen & Co., London. **2.**

266. Political and Economic Planning (1963) *Psychiatric Services in 1975,* Broadsheet, 29(468), London. **6, 21.**

267. Political and Economic Planning (1966) *Mental Sub-Normality in London: A Survey of Community Care.* London. **6, 21.**

268. Political and Economic Planning (1966) *Trends in Psychogeriatric Care,* Broadsheet, 32(497), London. **6, 10, 21.**

269. Pugh, E. (1968) *Social Work in Child Care,* Routledge & Kegan Paul, London. **2, 3, 28.**

270. Rehin, G.F. and Martin, F.M. (1968) *Patterns of Performance in Community Care,* Oxford University Press, London. **6, 21, 26.**

271. Residential Child Care Association (1968) *Residential Staff in Child Care* (Annual Review, Vol. 16). London. **28.**

272. Rice, A.K. (1963) *The Enterprise and its Environment,* Tavistock Publications, London. **18.**

273. Richardson, Helen J. (1969) *Adolescent Girls in Approved Schools,* Routledge & Kegan Paul, London. **3, 28.**

274. Robb, Barbara. (1967) *Sans Everything,* Nelson, London. **21, 28.**

275. Roberts, N. (1960) *Everybody's Business: The 1959 Mental Health Act and the Community,* National Association for Mental Health, London. **21.**

276. Roberts, N. (1961) *Not in My Perfect Mind - The Care of Mentally Frail Old People,* National Association for Mental Health, London. **6, 10, 21.**

277. Robson, William Alexander and Crick, Bernard (eds.) (1970) *The Future of the Social Services,* Penguin Books, Harmondsworth. **29.**

278. Rodgers, Barbara N. and Dixon, Julia. (1960) *Portrait of Social Work - A Study of Social Services in a Northern Town,* Oxford University Press, London. **3, 9, 10, 11, 12, 26, 29, 31**

279. Rooff, Madeline. (1957) *Voluntary Societies and Social Policy,* Routledge & Kegan Paul, London. **11, 19, 29, 31.**

280. Samuels, Alec. (1963) *Law for Social Workers,* Butterworth, London. **1, 3, 17, 21, 22.**

281. Schaffer, H.R. (1968) *Child Care and the Family: A Study of Short-Term Care* Occasional Papers on Social Administration, 25. G. Bell & Co., London. **3.**

282. Selltiz, Claire *et al.* (revised edition 1965) *Research Methods in Social Relations.* Methuen & Co., London. **27.**

283. Skinner, F.W. (1969) *Physical Disability and Community Care: A Study of the Prevalence and Nature of Disability in Relation to Environmental Characteristics and Social Services in a London Borough,* National Council of Social Service, London. **11.**

284. Skottowe, Philip F. (2nd edition 1967) *Law Relating to the Blind,* Butterworth, London. **17.**

285. Slack, K.M. (1960) *Councils, Committees and Concern for the Old: A Study of the Provision, Extent and Co-ordination of Certain Services for Old People in the County of London.* Occasional Papers on Social Administration, 2, Codicote Press, Welwyn, Herts. **10, 29.**

286. Slack, K.M. (ed.) (1964) *Some Aspects of Residential Care of the Elderly,* National Council of Social Service, London. (For National Old People's Welfare Council.) **10, 28.**

287. Slack, K.M. (1966) *Social Administration and the Citizen,* Michael Joseph, London (Bibliography). **29.**

288. Sparks, R.F. and Hood, R.G. (eds.) (1968) *The Residential Treatment of Disturbed and Delinquent Boys,* University of Cambridge, Institute of Criminology. **16, 28.**

289. Speller, S.R. (2nd revised edition 1964) *The Mental Health Act, 1959,* Institute of Hospital Administrators, London. **21.**

290. Stewart, J.D. (1969) *New Approaches to Management in Local Government,* Local Government Chronicle & Charles Knight, London. **18.**

291. Stroud, J.A. (1965) *An Introduction to the Child Care Service,* Education Today Series, Longmans, Green & Co., London. **3, 29.**

292. Sumner, Greta and Smith, Randall. (1969) *Planning Local Authority Services for the Elderly,* George Allen & Unwin, London. **10.**

293. Thomas, Edwin J. (1967) *Behavioral Science for Social Workers,* The Free Press, New York. **18, 26.**

294. Timms, Noel. (1964) *Psychiatric Social Work in Great Britain 1939-1962,* Routledge & Kegan Paul, London. **24, 29.**

295. Timms, Noel. (1964) *Social Casework – Principles and Practice,* Routledge & Kegan Paul, London. **2.**

296. Timms, Noel. (2nd edition 1969) *Casework in the Child Care Service,* Butterworth, London (Bibliography). **2, 3.**

297. Titmuss, Richard M. (1968) *Commitment to Welfare,* George Allen & Unwin, London. **6, 12, 29.**

298. Tizard, J. (1964) *Community Services for the Mentally Handicapped,* Oxford University Press, London (Bibliography). **6, 21, 28.**

299. Tizard, J. and Grad, J.C. (1961) *The Mentally Handicapped and Their Families: A Social Survey,* Oxford University Press, London. **6, 21, 26.**

300. Tod, Robert J.N. (ed.) (1968) *Children in Care* (Papers on Residential Work, Vol. I), Longmans, Green & Co., London. **3, 28.**

301. Tod, Robert J.N. (1968) *Disturbed Children* (Papers on Residential Work, Vol. 2), Longmans, Green & Co., London. **3, 21, 28.**

302. Todd, F. Joan. (1967) *Social Work with the Mentally Sub-normal,* Routledge & Kegan Paul, London (Bibliography). **6, 21.**

303. Townsend, Peter. (1961) *The Development of Home and Welfare Services for Old People, 1946-60,* Association of Directors of Welfare Services, Leicester. **10, 29.**

304. Townsend, Peter. (1962) *The Last Refuge - A Survey of Residential Institutions and Homes for the Aged in England and Wales,* Routledge & Kegan Paul, London. **10, 28.**
305. Townsend, Peter. (1963) *The Family Life of Old People,* Penguin Books, Harmondsworth (Bibliography). **10.**
306. Townsend, Peter and Wedderburn, Dorothy. (1965) *The Aged in the Welfare State.* G. Bell & Sons, London. (Includes list of Social Surveys of Old People 1945-64). **10, 26.**
307. Trasler, G.B. (1960) *In Place of Parents: A Study of Foster Care,* Routledge & Kegan Paul, London (Bibliography). **3.**
308. Trecker, Harleigh B. (1961) *New Understandings of Administration,* Association Press, New York. **18, 29.**
309. Tripodi, Tony; Fellin, Phillip; Meyer, Henry J. (1969) *The Assessment of Social Research.* F. E. Peacock, Itasca, Ill. **26.**
310. Tunstall, Jeremy. (1966) *Old and Alone,* Routledge & Kegan Paul, London (Bibliography). **10, 26.**
311. United Nations - European Social Development Programme 1970 *(Report of Study Group on the Meaning and Implications of Community Care),* New York. **3, 6, 20, 31.**
312. Warham, Joyce. (1967) *An Introduction to Administration for Social Workers,* Routledge & Kegan Paul, London (Bibliography). **18.**
313. West, D.J. (1967) *The Young Offender,* Penguin Books, Harmondsworth (Bibliography). **16.**
314. Whitehead, A. (1970) *In the Service of Old Age: The Welfare of Psychogeriatric Patients,* Penguin Books, Harmondsworth. **10, 21.**
315. Wilensky, Harold L. and Lebeaux, Charles N. (1958) *Industrial Society and Social Welfare,* Russell Sage Foundation, New York. **18, 29.**
316. Willmott, Phyllis, (1967) *Consumers' Guide to the British Social Services,* Penguin Books, Harmondsworth. **25.**
317. Willson, F.M.G. (1961) *Administrators in Action - British Case Studies,* George Allen & Unwin, London (especially Chapter V). **3, 18, 29.**
318. Winnicott, Clare. (1964) *Child Care and Social Work* - A Collection of Papers written between 1954 and 1963, Codicote Press, Welwyn, Herts. **2, 3.**
319. Winnicott, D.W. (1965) *The Family and Individual Development,* Tavistock Publications. London. **2, 4, 21.**
320. Woodroofe, Kathleen. (1962) *From Charity to Social Work in England and the United States,* Routledge & Kegan Paul, London. **29.**
321. Working Party on the Social Work (Scotland) Act, 1968 (1969) *Social Work in Scotland,* Edinburgh University, Department of Social Administration. **3, 10, 11, 18, 20, 21, 28, 29, 30.**
322. Young, A.F. and Ashton, E.T. (1956) *British Social Work in the Nineteenth Century,* Routledge & Kegan Paul, London. **6, 11, 22, 28, 29.**
323. Young, Priscilla. (1967) *The Student and Supervision in Social Work Education.* Routledge & Kegan Paul, London. **30.**
324. Young, Priscilla *et al.* (1968) *Administration and Staff Supervision in the Child Care Service,* Monograph, 2, Association of Child Care Officers, London. **3, 18.**
325. Younghusband, Eileen. (1964) *Social Work and Social Change,* George Allen & Unwin, London. **16, 22, 29, 30**
326. Younghusband, Eileen (ed.). (1966) *New Developments in Casework,* George Allen & Unwin, London. **2.**
327. Younghusband, Eileen. (ed.) (1967) *Social Work and Social Values* - Readings in Social Work, Vol. III, George Allen & Unwin, London. **2, 3, 20, 29.**
328. Younghusband, Eileen. (ed.) (1968) *Education for Social Work,* George

Allen & Unwin, London. **30.**

329. Younghusband, Eileen *et al.* (eds.) (1970) *Living with Handicap: the Report of a Working Party on Children with Special Needs,* National Bureau for Co-operation in Child Care, London. **3, 11.**

C. JOURNAL ARTICLES

330. ADMINISTRATIVE and Social Work Problems of Services for the Handicapped. Potter, R.S.J. (1966) *Social Work,* 23, 4. 3-9. **11, 18, 29.**
331. The ADMINISTRATIVE Structure of the Child Guidance Service: An Historical Note. Ryan, T.M. (1967) *Social Work,* 24, 3. 23-27. **18, 21, 29.**
332. The APPLICATION of Management Theory to the Social Services. Ashton, E.T. (1967) *Social Work,* 24, 2, (April). 3-8. **18.**
333. BUREAUCRATIC and Professional Orientation Patterns in Social Casework. Billingsley, A. (1964) *Social Service Review,* 38 (December). **18.**
334. A CASE-STUDY in the Functioning of Social Systems as a Defence against Anxiety. Menzies, Isabel E.P. (1960) *Human Relations.* 13, 2. 95-121. **18, 28.**
335. CASEWORK with the Ageing. *Social Casework* (1961) Special Issue – 42 (5 and 6). **2, 10.**
336. CHILD Care and a Social Service Department. Kahan, Barbara (1968) *Social Work,* 25, 4. 9-14. **3, 18.**
337. CHILDREN and Young Persons Act, 1969. Form and Context of Regional Plan. Direction Given by the Secretary of State in Exercise of the Powers conferred by Section 36(6) of the Act. (Text of Circular on the Regional Plan and the Memorandum of Guidance). *Child Care News,* 102, September, 1970. 7-13. **17.**
338. CHILDREN and Young Persons in Need of Care, Protection or Control. Strachan, Billy (1965) *Justice of the Peace and Local Government Review,* 6 February. **3, 16, 17.**
339. COMMUNITY Mental Health Agency and the Aged. Roy, R.G. (1969) *Case Conference,* 16, 5, (September). 178-181. **10, 18, 21.**
340. The CONCEPT of Role-Filling and its Use for the Social Work Administrator. Brown, M.J. (1969) *Case Conference,* 16, 4. 143-145. **18.**
341. CORPORATE Responsibility in Local Government. Stewart, J.D. (1969) *Local Government Chronicle,* 5336, 7 June. 1039-1040. **18.**
342. DEALING with Children in Trouble. Boss, Peter (1968) *Case Conference,* 15, 3, (July). 86-89. **3, 17.**
343. DIVISIVE Integration. Senior, Derek (1970) *Local Government Chronicle,* 5373, 21 February. **12, 18.**
344. EVIDENCE to the Seebohm Committee on Local Authority and Allied Personal Social Services. Institute of Housing Managers. *Housing,* 11. January, 1967. 13-15. **14.**
345. EXPERIMENTS in Welfare. *Trends in Education,* January, 1969. 10-13. **9.**
346. FAMILY Advice Service. Leissner, Aryeh (1969) *British Hospital Journal,* LXXIX, 4109, 17 January. 120-122. **18.**
347. FEWER Children for Court – A Guide to the Children and Young Persons Act, 1969. *New Society,* 15, 379, 1 January, 1970. **3, 16, 17.**
348. FINANCING the New Social Service Department. *Rating and Valuation Reporter,* 1 August, 1968. 481-482. **18.**
349. The FUTURE Organisation of the Social Services. Rodgers, B. (1968/69) *Manchester Literary and Philosophical Society Memoirs and Proceedings,* 111. 5-26. **18.**
350. The MAKING of a Department. Hopkins, J.S. (1967) *Case Conference,* 14, 7. **3, 18, 29.**

351. MANAGEMENT and Organisation in the Social Services. Algie, J. (1970) *British Hospital Journal,* LXXX, 4184. 1245-1248. **18.**

352. MANAGEMENT by Objectives in an Education Department. Mann, John (1970) *Local Government Chronicle,* 31 October. 2209-2210. **18.**

353. MANAGEMENT Education in Local Government. Stewart, J.D. (1970) *Local Government Chronicle,* 5373, 21 February. **30.**

354. MANAGEMENT in Social Service. Barter, John (1969) *British Hospital Journal,* LXXIX, 4132. 1220-1221. **18.**

355. The NEED for a Social Plan. Townsend, P. (1967) *New Society,* 14 December. 852-855. **18.**

356. A NEW Portrait of Social Work, Rodgers, Barbara N. (1970) *Social and Economic Administration,* 4, 3. 186-193. **18.**

357. ORGANISATION of Children's Departments. Rowbottom, Ralph; Seed, Helen; and Davidson, Lillien (1970) *Local Government Chronicle,* 5374, 28 February. 429-435. **3, 18.**

358. The ORGANISATION of Community Health and Welfare Services. Jefferys, Margot (1965) *Social Work,* 22, 2-3. 19-21 & 28. **6, 18.**

359. ORGANISATIONAL Problems in Setting Up a Local Authority Social Services Department. Brown, M. and Foren, R. (1970) *Local Government Chronicle,* 5395, 25 July. 1497-1500. **18.**

360. OVERLAPPING and Co-operation. Wedge, P.J. (1967) *New Society,* 27 July. 120-121. **18.**

361. PLANNING and Social Services. Baker, S.H. (1968) *Town Planning Inst. Journal,* 54, December. 479. **18.**

362. The PRACTICE of Psychiatric Social Work and the Future of the Child Guidance Clinic. Rehin, G.F. (1969) *Case Conference,* 16, 2, (June). 42-47. **18, 24, 26.**

363. PROFILE of an Urban Area. McCulloch, J.W. and Brown, M. (1970) *Municipal Review,* 41, 483, (March). **27.**

364. PSYCHOLOGICAL Problems in the Social Services. Foren, R. and Brown, M. (1970) *British Hospital Journal,* LXXX, 4194, 5 September. 1739. **18.**

365. REACTION to Change in Social Service Departments. Davies, Conway (1968) *Case Conference.* 14, 9, (January). 331-334. **18.**

366. RECENT Developments in Social Work – A Survey Article. Forder, Anthony and Kay, Sheila (1969) *Social and Economic Administration.* 3, 2. (Bibliography). **2, 29.**

367. RE-ORGANISATION of a Health and Welfare Department. Knight, G.W. (1967) *Case Conference,* 13, 11, (March). 379-384 and 393. **18.**

368. SCHOOLS and the Social Service Department. Plowden, Lady Bridget (1968) *Social Work,* 25, 4. 33-37. **9, 18.**

369. SEEBOHM: Lambeth Style. Baines, David (1970) *British Hospital Journal,* LXXX, 4187, 17 July. 1393-1395. **18.**

370. SEEBOHM: Organisational Problems and Policy Proposals. Part One. Spencer, Claudine (1970) *Social and Economic Administration,* 4, 3. 172-185. **18.**

371. The SEEBOHM Report and Social Work Education. Stevenson, Olive (1968) *Social Work,* 25, 4. 28-32. **30.**

372. SOCIAL Administration and Scarcity: The Problem of Rationing. Parker, R.A. (1967) *Social Work,* 24, 2, (April). 9-14. **18.**

373. SOCIAL Priority Areas and Seebohm. Deacon, Bob and Cannan, Crescy (1970) *Social Work Today,* 1, 6. 44-53. **18, 26.**

374. The SOCIAL Services and Local Government Reform. White, Tom (1968) *Case Conference,* 15, 5. **29.**

375. SOCIAL Work in the 70's. Holman, Robert and Radford, Elizabeth (1969) *British Hospital Journal,* LXXIX, 4134, 1312-1313. **30.**

376. SOCIAL Work Organisations – New Models for Old. Hopkins, Jeff. (1969) *Case Conference,* 16, 8, (December). 306-311. **18.**
377. SOCIAL Workers in Local Government. Parker, Julia and Allen, Rosalind (1969) *Social and Economic Administration,* 3, 1. **18, 26.**
378. SOME Thoughts on Performance Assessment. Edwards, Fred. (1969) *Case Conference,* 16, 8. **18, 30.**
379. SPECIALISATION within a Unified Social Service. Stevenson, Olive (1968) *Case Conference,* 15, 5, (September). 184-189. **18.**
380. STRUCTURAL Conflict in Social Work. Hopkins, Jeff. (1966) *Case Conference,* 13, 7, (November). 254-255. **18.**
381. STRUCTURING a Social Services Department. (By a Welfare Officer.) (1970) *British Hospital Journal,* LXXX, 4186, 10 July. 1345-1346. **18.**
382. STUDYING and Creating Change: a Means to Understanding Social Organisation. Mann, F.C. (1957) *Research in Industrial Human Relations,* 17. **18.**
383. SYSTEMATIC Decision Making in the Child Care Service: Attitudes Reflected in Three Research Seminars. Williams, Allan P.O. (1968) *Social Work,* 25, 2. 3-6. **18.**
384. TASKS Ahead of an Integrated Social Work Department. De Gruchy, Stella (1970) *Case Conference,* 16, 10. 397-401. **18.**
385. THOUGHTS on Management Services Units. Stewart, J.D. (1969) *Local Government Chronicle,* 5360, 22 November. 2211-2212. **18.**
386. TOWARDS an Organisation of Social Services Departments. Rowbottom, Ralph and Hey, Anthea (1970) *Local Government Chronicle,* 5403, 19 September. 1849-1855. **18.**
387. TOWARDS Integrated Social Work Departments. Jones, David (1970) *Social Work Today,* 1, 1. 22-24. **18.**
388. TRAINING for Management in the Social Services. Crichton, Anne (1967) *Social Work,* 24, 2, (April). 20-26. **18, 30.**
389. USE of Social Indices in Psychiatric Epidemiology. McCulloch, J.W. and Philip, A.E. (1966) *British Journal of Preventive and Social Medicine,* 20, 3, (July). **27.**
390. WELFARE Departments and Territorial Justice: Some Implications for the Reform of Local Government. Davies, Bleddyn (1969) *Social and Economic Administration,* 3, 4. **18, 29, 30.**
391. WHAT to do about Planned Programme Budgeting. Ward, R.A. and Harris, P. (1970) *Local Government Chronicle,* 5402, 12 September. 1796-1797. **18.**
392. The WORK of Two Children's Departments. George, Vic and Hazel, Nancy (1970) *Social Work,* 27, 1. 23-25. **3, 26.**

D. COMMENT AND OPINION

393. ADAPTING to Change. Newton, George (1968) *Social Work,* 25, 1. 3-7
394. An AMERICAN View. Perlman, Robert (1968) *Social Work,* 25, 4. 38-41.
395. APRON Strings – New Style. Editorial (1970) *Local Government Chronicle,* 21 April.
396. ARE We back to Square One? *Times Educational Supplement,* 24 January, 1969. 230
397. CALL to Delay Social Services Re-organisation. (By Rural District Councils Association and Association of Municipal Corporations) *Municipal Journal,* 2 August, 1968. 1878.

398. CHILDREN'S Officers. (Review of evidence of Association of Children's Officers submitted to Seebohm Committee) *Teachers' World,* 7 October, 1966. 51-52.
399. CHOOSING Scottish Welfare Principal Officers. *Municipal Journal,* 17 January, 1969. 121-122
400. CHRONICALLY Sick and Disabled Persons Act, 1970. Raven, Helena (1970) *Social Work Today,* 1, 5. 15-17.
401. CIVIC Rights and Social Services. Brooke, R. (1969) *Political Quarterly* 40, 1. 90-102.
402. COMMITTEE on Local Authority and Allied Personal Social Services: Second Supplementary Memorandum. The Association of Municipal Corporations. *Municipal Review,* 38, May, 1967. Supplement, 150-153.
403. COMMUNITY Careless. Lapping, A. (1970) *New Society,* 9 April. 589-591.
404. CONTEXT of Local Authority Personal Services. (Sir Keith Joseph's speech to Conference of Children's Officers) *Local Government Finance,* January, 1968. 6-10.
405. DOCTOR or Social Worker? *British Medical Journal,* 3 August, 1968. 265-266.
406. FAMILY Welfare and Seebohm. Townsend, P. (1968) *New Society,* 1 August. 159-160.
407. The FUTURE of the Personal Social Services. Parker, R.A. (1969) *Political Quarterly,* 40, 1. 47-55.
408. FUTURE of the Social Services. *Local Government Finance,* October, 1966. 365-371.
409. GIVE Home Helps New Status. (By a Welfare Officer) (1969) *Municipal Journal,* 16 May. 1251.
410. GO-SLOW on Seebohm. Lapping, B. (1969) *New Society,* 13, 332, 6 February. 208-209.
411. HEALTH and Social Services of the Future. *Local Government Finance,* October, 1968. 365-369.
412. HEALTH and Welfare Re-organisation. French, Cecil W. (1969) *British Hospital Journal,* LXXIX, 4107, 3 January. 31.
413. HEALTH and Welfare – The Long Haul. Mair, R. (1969) *Municipal Review,* May. 244-246.
414. HOME Help Service in Changing Times. (By a Welfare Officer) (1970) *Municipal Journal,* 27 February. 500.
415. IN or Out? – An Agonising Appraisal. Jarvis, F.V. (1967) *Case Conference,* 14, 4, (August). 137-143.
416. The INFLEXIBLE System of Social Services. Liddiard, R. (1969) *Municipal Journal,* 12 December. 3110-3111.
417. LET Councils Pick Seebohm Chiefs. *Municipal Journal,* 23 May, 1969. 1310.
418. The LOCAL Authority Social Services Bill. Comments from Three Social Workers (1970) *Social Work,* 27, 2. 3-6.
419. A LONG Way from the Soup Kitchen. Jeger, L. (1968) *New Statesman,* 76, 2 August. 133.
420. A LOOK Back or a Step Forward. Elliott, A. (1968) *Social Work,* 25, 4. 19-22.
421. MAKING Best Use of the Welfare Budget. *New Society,* 5 August, 1965. 6-7.
422. MAKING Seebohm Work. Vernon, Betty (1970) *British Hospital Journal,* LXXX, 4179, 22 May. 975.
423. MEDICAL and Social Welfare. (Observations on some of the factors under consideration by Seebohm Committee) *British Medical Journal,* 19 November, 1966. 1216-1217.

424. MEDICAL and Social Work Practice in the Local Authority. Kahn, J.H. (1967) *Case Conference*, 13, 11, (March). 385-388.
425. MEDICAL Opinion on Seebohm Proposals. (By a Medical Officer of Health) (1969) *Municipal Journal*, 25 April. 1041-1043.
426. A MINISTRY of Social Welfare? Lapping, A. (1968) *New Society*, 11, 23 May. 748-749.
427. Mr. SEEBOHM Urges Early Action. *Municipal Journal*, 9 May, 1969. 1173.
428. NEED, Scarce Resources and Rationing. Hardy, Jean (1970) *British Hospital Journal*, LXXX, 4188, 24 July. 1443-1444.
429. A NEW Role for Local Authorities. (Implications of the Chronically Sick and Disabled Persons Act). By a Welfare Officer. (1970) *Local Government Chronicle*, 5401, 5 September. 1759-1760.
430. NOT Enough Staff for the Work Load. (By a Welfare Officer). (1968) *Municipal Journal*, 16 August. 1987.
431. ONWARDS with Seebohm. Beglin, M.F. (1968) *Local Government Chronicle*, 3 August. 1191-1192.
432. OPEN Letter to a Director of Social Services. Smith, Jeff (1970) *British Hospital Journal*, LXXX, 4196, 19 September. 1840-1841.
433. OTHER Side of the Home Help Picture. (By a Senior Home Help Organiser) (1969) *Municipal Journal*, 18 July. 1845.
434. PLANNERS and the Seebohm Report. Harbert, W.B. (1968) *Town and Country Planning*, 36, December. 523-525.
435. The POLITICAL Economy of Social Services. Wiseman, J. (1965) *Listener*, 74, 7 October. 515-517.
436. QUID Pro Quo on Seebohm? Association of Health Administrative Officers *Local Government Chronicle*, 5352, 27 September, 1969. 1781.
437. REACTIONARY Past? Radical Future? Price, J.R. (1968) *British Hospital Journal*, 6 December. 2285-2286.
438. REFORM of the Welfare Services. Mair, Robert (1969) *Social Service Quarterly*, XLIII, 2. 62-65.
439. RE-ORGANISING Social Welfare. Brown, M. (1965) *New Society*, 30 December. 15.
440. REPORT of the Committee on Local Authority and Allied Social Services. Statement by the Institute of Housing Managers *Housing*, 4 March, 1969. 21-22.
441. The ROLE of Local Authorities in Welfare – Seebohm outlines shortcomings. *Local Government Chronicle*, 14 December, 1968. 1988.
442. The ROLE of the Social Services. Marshall, T.H. (1969) *Political Quarterly*, 40, 1. 1-11.
443. SCOTTISH Experience and its Implications for Medical Social Workers. McInnes, M. (1969) *Medical Social Work*, 22, May. 34-41.
444. The SCOTTISH White Paper – 'Social Work and the Community'. Mack, J.A. (1967) *British Journal of Criminology*, 7, (July). 336-339.
445. SEEBOHM: A Painful Dilemma for the Probation Service. Murch, M. (1969) *Probation*, 15, (March). 18-23.
446. SEEBOHM and the Commentators. Wrigley, Sir J. (1968/69) *Social Service Quarterly*, Winter. 79-82.
447. The SEEBOHM Committee Report – a Great State Paper. Cormack, Una. (1969) *Social and Economic Administration*, 3, 1. 52-61.
448. SEEBOHM Danger to School Welfare? *Municipal Journal*, 11 April, 1969. 904.
449. SEEBOHM on Seebohm. Seebohm, F. (1968) *Local Government Chronicle*, 5305, 2 November. 1741.
450. SEEBOHM Pinpoints gaps in Welfare. (By a Welfare Officer.) (1968) *Municipal Journal*, 2 August. 1875.

Appendix: Bibliography

451. SEEBOHM Report. Burnett, Margaret (1968) *Medical Social Work,* 21, 5, 131-136.
452. SEEBOHM Report. Lloyd, P.L. (1968) *LGA, The Journal of the Institute of Local Government Administrators,* 9 November. 15-20.
453. SEEBOHM Report 'A Damp Squib'. (By a Housing Manager) *Municipal Journal,* 10 January, 1969. 70-71.
    Criticised by – The DAMP Squib Explodes: Defence of Seebohm. Moulton, Leonard. (1969) *Municipal Journal,* 24 January. 175; 31 January. 237.
454. SEEBOHM Report and the Future Role of the Voluntary Bodies. Owens, J.K. (1969) *Social Service Quarterly,* Spring. 131-135.
455. SEEBOHM Report: Its Implications for Housing Managers. *Housing,* 4, September, 1968. 3-4.
456. SEEBOHM – The Recommendations. *Local Government Chronicle,* 27 July, 1968. 1141-1142.
457. SEEBOHM: The Report and its Implications. Donnison, D.V. (1968) *Social Work,* 25, 4, (October). 3-8.
458. SEEBOHM – Who Cares? Lillington, B.R. and Smith, M.E. (1969) *Case Conference,* 16, 2, (June). 53-56.
459. SEEBOHM's Amputation – Robinson's Fusion. *Public Health,* September, 1968. 244-252.
460. SOCIAL Services Reform – England and Wales. *Public Health,* March, 1967. 102-108.
461. A SOCIAL Work Amalgamation. Page, I. (1968) *New Society,* 31 October, 639-640.
462. SOCIAL Work and the Community: Notes on the Scottish White Paper. Jones, David (1967) *Social Work,* 24, 1. 25-27.
463. SOCIAL Work Tomorrow – Scotland's Challenges. Richards, K. (1968) *Medical Social Work,* 21, 4. 101-107.
464. SOCIAL Worker as Jack of all Trades. (By a Welfare Officer) (1968) *Municipal Journal,* 9 August. 1934-1935.
465. SOME Reflections on Working in a Combined Social Service Agency in a Local Authority Setting in Canada. Thorburn, June (1969) *Case Conference,* 15, 12, (April). 478-482.
466. SOME Thoughts on Child Guidance Clinics and the Future Social Service Departments. Briskin, Sidney I. (1970) *Social Work Today,* 1, 7. 12-16.
467. THOUGHTS on Seebohm and Housing Management. Bennett, L.C. (1968) *Housing,* November. 56.
468. TIME for Change. (Summaries of papers presented by Lord Kilbrandon and Mr. F. Seebohm at the annual conference of the Association of Children's Officers) *British Hospital Journal,* 1 November, 1968. 2060-2061.
469. UNIVERSALITY Versus Selectivity. Reddin, M. (1969) *Political Quarterly,* 40, 1. 12-22.
470. A VIEW from the Probation Service. Jarvis, F.V. (1968) *Social Work,* 25, 4. 15-18.
471. WELFARE Services and the Social Welfare Department. Speed, M.G. (1968) *Social Work,* 25, 4. 23-27.
472. A WELFARE Service Not a Welfare Department. Brown, Muriel (1966) *Social Service Quarterly,* XXXIX, 3. 91-94.
473. WHAT'S Wrong with the Social Services? Kent, B. (1967) *Case Conference,* 13, 11, (March). 375-378.